University of Cambridge

Department of Applied Economics

OCCASIONAL PAPERS

8

Productivity in Distribution

by K. D. GEORGE

CAMBRIDGE UNIVERSITY PRESS

Price 15s. net in U.K.;

$3. 00 in U.S.A.

University of Cambridge
Department of Applied Economics
OCCASIONAL PAPERS 8

PRODUCTIVITY IN DISTRIBUTION

University of Cambridge

Department of Applied Economics

Occasional Papers

Productivity in Distribution

by K. D. GEORGE

Department of Applied Economics
and Sidney Sussex College, Cambridge

CAMBRIDGE

AT THE UNIVERSITY PRESS

1966

PUBLISHED BY

THE SYNDICS OF THE CAMBRIDGE UNIVERSITY PRESS

Bentley House, 200 Euston Road, London, N.W.1.

American Branch: 32 East 57th Street, New York, N.Y. 10022

West African Office: P.M.B. 5181, Ibadan, Nigeria

PRODUCED BY UNEOPRINT
set on electric keyboards
photo-reproduced and printed offset
at The Gresham Press
UNWIN BROTHERS LIMITED
Old Woking Surrey England

Contents

HF
5349
G7
G4

LIST OF TABLES

Preface

This Paper is one of the fruits of the early stages of research into productivity in the service industries undertaken in the Department of Applied Economics. It is a cross section study of sales, employment and productivity in retailing, based on the 1961 Census of Distribution.

The analysis is largely on a town basis. The composition of sales, characteristics of the labour force, and labour productivity, are compared between towns of different sizes and between towns having a similar size of market. The Paper examines such questions as 'do large towns have a higher productivity than small ones—either for all shops together or in particular kinds of business?'; 'is part-time labour mainly used in towns where labour is scarce and does it help to raise productivity?'; 'how far can multiple regression techniques explain differences in productivity by reference to such factors as different degrees of excess demand for labour, size of shop, and income per head?'

It is difficult in any research in applied economics to arrive at unambiguous conclusions and to prove the existence of causal relationships in the data under examination. This certainly applies to the present Paper but it is also fair to say that the results are far more striking than the author had anticipated in the early stages of research.

The research has involved a considerable amount of work in extracting, transforming and analysing data. I am indebted to Miss Marion Clarke and her assistants for carrying out what must have seemed to them to be an endless number of computations; to Mrs. Valerie Lea for preparing the data for the computor; to the Board of Trade Census Office for some unpublished information obtained in the 1961 Census of Distribution, and to the Ministry of Labour for allowing me to extract from their files the information on the state of the labour market in the towns included in the analysis. I would also like to thank Mrs. Silk and her staff for typing various versions of the manuscript.

During the course of the work I have benefited from discussions with Mr. Aubrey Silberston and Mr. B. M. Deakin, and Mr. Ajit Singh has given advice on a number of statistical points.

I should like in particular to express my gratitude to Mr. W. B. Reddaway, the Director of the Department of Applied Economics. It was he who originated the 'service industries' project, and all along he has been unstinting with his valuable advice. Needless to say, I am solely responsible for any errors and for the shortcomings of the analysis.

K. D. G.

University of Cambridge
Department of Applied Economics

June 1966

9

Introduction

n 1964 3. 4 million workers, or fourteen per cent of the total work-force
n civil employment in Great Britain were engaged in the Distributive
Trades, and of these approximately three quarters i.e. 2. 5 million were
engaged in retailing. It is a commonly expressed view that the performance
of the Distributive Trades in terms of labour productivity is poor compared, say, to productivity in manufacturing. There does indeed appear to
be great scope for improvement in a sector of the economy which is
dominated by small traders and where the introduction of new methods of
wholesaling and retailing are still in the early stages of development. In
any event, in a period of general labour shortage the degree of efficiency
n the use of labour in transferring goods from producers to consumers
s of particular importance.

Some recent research on productivity
in distribution

Some recent publications on productivity have been concerned, among
other things, with the rate of growth of output per man, and with the
relative performance in this respect of different sectors of the economy.
n a comparison of the inter-war and post-war years C. H. Feinstein
found that the faster rate of growth in output per man-year in the latter
period owed very little to a rise in the rate for Industrial Production and
was to be attributed almost entirely to the service industries. (1) For the
Distributive Trades output per man-year decreased by sixteen per cent
between 1924 and 1937 but increased by sixteen per cent between 1948
and 1962. The fact that during the inter-war period employment in distribution grew so much faster than output can be explained by the movement of labour from the industrial to the service sector of the economy
as a result of the high level of unemployment. The annual rate of growth
of employment in the Distributive Trades between 1924 and 1937 was 2. 6
per cent compared to an annual rate of growth of output of 2. 0 per cent.
n the period 1948-1962 the low level of unemployment has been associated with a much lower rate of increase in employment in distribution;
. 7 per cent per annum, compared to an annual rate of growth of output
of 2. 8 per cent. (2)

---

1) C. H. Feinstein: Production and Productivity 1920-1962. London
   and Cambridge Economic Bulletin, December 1963.

2) The figures in this paragraph refer to Distributive Trades, but
   with retailing accounting for three quarters of this sector in terms
   of employment, they also reflect the general change which has occurred in the retail trades only.

The question has been posed (1) as to whether the improved performan of the Distributive Trades in terms of labour productivity has been a once for all gain or whether the new labour market conditions will lead to continued advance being made. Evidence to support the latter view i given by Lady Margaret Hall. (2) Using Census of Distribution data Lac Hall finds that from 1957 to 1961 output per man in retail trade increa at a rate of 2.9 per cent per annum, compared to 1.5 to 2.0 per cent p annum for the period 1950 to 1957.

The rate of increase in labour productivity in retailing showed a mark improvement then in the post-war as compared to the inter-war years and within the post-war period there is evidence of an acceleration in the rate of increase. We do not intend in this Paper to pursue any further the question of productivity changes over time. Having sketched very briefly the average improvements that have taken place in labour productivity we now concern ourselves, by means of a cross-section analysis based on the 1961 Census of Distribution, with the question of the extent to which performance in retailing varied in 1961. In other words, to what extent did the labour productivity of the majority of retailers measure up to that of the best in 1961? And what factors were associated with the productivity differences that existed?

A regional comparison of labour productivity

The above questions can be looked at on a regional basis. Table 1.1 gives a regional comparison of total retail sales per person engaged. The regions are arranged in descending order of the value of sales per person engaged, and the figure for the South Western region at the bottom of the list is sixteen per cent lower than that for the London and South Eastern region which is at the top. For six regions, sales per person engaged are fourteen per cent or more lower than they are for London and the South East.

There also appears to be a rough association between sales per person engaged and the 'explanatory' factors—the degree of tightness in the labour market as measured by the percentage of the workforce unemployed, income per head, and sales size of shop. The regions with relatively high sales per person engaged tend to have a lower percentage of unemployment, higher income per head and a larger sales size of shop than the regions with relatively low sales per person engaged.

Although these relationships are certainly interesting it would seem more fruitful to pursue the analysis of variations in labour productivity on a town rather than on a regional basis for the following reasons.

---

(1) R. C. O. Matthews, Some Aspects of Post-War Growth in the British Economy in Relation to Historical Experience, p. 20. Paper read to the Manchester Statistical Society, November 1964.

(2) Developments in British Retailing Since 1957. London and Cambridge Economic Bulletin, December 1963.

Table 1.1. British Retail Trade 1961. Sales per Person Engaged and Certain Explanatory Factors. By Region

Region	Sales per person engaged* (FTE)§ £	% of work-force unemployed† (ave. 1957-61) %	Income per head‡ 1960 £	Sales per shop* £
London and S. E.	4506	1.1	812	19,881
Midland	4222	1.3	752	14,812
Eastern	4203	1.2	715	16,709
Southern	4050	1.3	733	18,442
N. Midland	4015	1.1	718	13,545
East and West Ridings	3892	1.4	712	13,142
Northern	3875	2.5	686	15,426
Scotland	3837	3.3	674	16,300
Wales	3813	3.2	678	12,600
North Western	3798	2.2	709	11,754
South Western	3783	1.8	691	14,990
Great Britain	4070	1.7	734	15,449

Sources   * Census of Distribution 1961.
           † Ministry of Labour Gazette.
           ‡ From the 106th Report of the Commissioners of Her
             Majesty's Inland Revenue, Table 76.

Note   § Equals full-time equivalent, two part-time workers
             being counted as equivalent to one full-time worker.

First, it is desirable to conduct the comparisons of labour productivity on the basis of units which give a reasonable degree of equality and homogeneity in the conditions of retailing. On a regional basis there are wide differences in such factors as the percentage of the population living in urban areas, and part of the difference in productivity between regions will be attributable to such factors. But differences in the degree of urbanisation will also, —because for instance of differences in population density and population structure, —affect the structure of shops, the pattern of demand and the amount of service which is associated with the sale of commodities, and these are factors which are not easily allowed for in a general study of productivity. On a town basis, however, Britain is a sufficiently homogeneous place to make it reasonable to assume that both the product mix and the amount of service associated with the sale of a given collection of commodities is, for any type of shop, fairly uniform from one town to another. This analysis then is concerned with differences in labour productivity between towns of a similar size where conditions of retailing are more uniform than they are on a regional basis.

Secondly, the town is a better approximation to the 'market' in retailing than is the region. It is difficult to identify the boundaries of a retailer' market. Any retailer will be faced with rivals who are nearer to him and others who are farther away, and the various retail markets are themselves linked. Furthermore, the boundaries of the market will vary from one kind of business to another being more distant for goods such as clothing and furniture than for the grocery trades. But the intensity of competition is greater at the town level than for regions so that any differences in productivity caused by differing degrees of competition are most likely to be revealed here.

Thirdly, the broad averages of regional figures will conceal larger differences both in labour productivity and in the variables used to explain differences in labour productivity. The real extent of the differences in productivity and the influence of the explanatory variables is more likely to be shown on a town than on a regional basis.

Finally, the greater number of towns than of regions gives greater scope for statistical analysis.

Main objectives of this Paper

The main objective of this Paper then is to examine productivity in retailing by a cross-section analysis, i.e. by studying inter-town differences in labour productivity as measured by sales per person engaged. The objectives, and to some extent the methods, can be seen by listing the types of questions to which we set out to find some sort of answer.

First, we set out to find the size of the differences between towns in the level of sales per person engaged. There obviously would be differences but we were concerned with whether these were large enough to be of much interest.

Secondly, we wanted to see whether the differences in labour productivity conformed to any systematic patterns. Does productivity, for example, tend to be higher for large towns than for small ones? Or do individual towns of much the same size show differences in productivity which are much more important than any general tendency for productivity to vary with size of town?

Thirdly, we wanted to see whether differences in productivity between towns of much the same size could be related to some other systematic factors such as the tightness of the labour market in the town, or the size of shop, or the proportion of the town's sales done by multiple shops.

Finally we wanted to examine the extent to which a multiple regression analysis, by reference to such factors as the tightness of the labour market, income per head and size of shop would give a statistical explanation of differences in productivity between towns.

14

1. Form of organisation

The above set of questions relates to sales by all forms of organisation. The analysis can be extended by distinguishing between 'independent' shops and 'multiples and cooperatives'. (1) Such questions as the following then arise: Does the percentage of sales attributable to multiples and co-operatives vary in any systematic way either between towns of different sizes or between towns within given size classes? If so, how can these variations be explained? And how far do the variations in the percentage of sales attributable to multiples and co-operatives go in explaining the variations in productivity between towns? We also wanted to see whether, for towns of much the same size, the degree of variation in labour productivity was much the same for both forms of organisation.

2. Kind of Business

A further extension of the analysis can be obtained by a breakdown of total retail sales into sales by different kinds of business—Groceries and Provisions, Clothing and Footwear etc. We wanted to see for instance whether the relationship between productivity and size of town differed for different kinds of business. We were also interested to see whether towns with a high over-all level of productivity would have a high level in each of the major kinds of business, and similarly for the lower end of the productivity scale. In any case we wanted to find out whether the patterns of variation in labour productivity which did emerge for the individual kinds of business could be explained by the sort of analysis indicated above for total retail sales, and to compare, for example, the apparent importance of labour shortage as an explanatory factor for groceries and clothing and footwear.

3. Central Shopping Areas

The 1961 Census of Distribution distinguishes retail trade in the main shopping centres within towns. (2) This allows such questions to be asked as; is there a relationship between the productivity of towns and the proportion of sales made in central shopping areas either between towns of very different size or between towns of much the same size? Is the central shopping area superior to the rest of the town in terms of labour productivity, or, since such a superiority is likely to be found, is it greatest

---

(1) 'Multiples' are organisations having 5 or more branches. We are not able in this analysis to distinguish between multiple organisations and co-operative societies because for a large number of towns separate figures are not given in the published reports of the 1961 Census of Distribution.

(2) The limits of shopping areas were defined as "where shops give way to residential property, or where lines of shops thin out and become interspersed with private dwellings; where this occurred, the limit was taken where the ratio of shops to all properties fell below one in three". See Report on the Census of Distribution and Other Services, Part 2, p. 6.

in high or low productivity towns? And is the superiority of high productivity over low productivity towns most marked inside the central
shopping area or in the rest of the town? These questions are asked in
respect of all retail trade and of individual kinds of business.

4. Part-time labour

An important characteristic of the labour market in the retail trades is
the extensive use which is made of part-time labour. We were particularly interested to see whether part-time labour is mainly used in towns
where labour is scarce, and in whether the use of part-time labour help
to raise productivity.

Towns included in the analysis

One hundred and sixty towns are included in the analysis, that is, all the
towns in Great Britain outside the County of London with sales exceedi
£10 million in 1961. The towns are grouped into five size-classes as
shown in Table 1. 2. The division is basically a compromise of the con-
flicting needs of maintaining as much uniformity as possible in the volu
of sales within any given size-class, and of having a sufficient number o
towns in each class to make the analysis sufficiently interesting statistically.

Table 1. 2.   Towns Included in the Analysis: by Size-Class

Size-Class	£ million sales 1961	Number of Towns
(1)	10 < 12. 25	31
(2)	12. 25 < 15	31
(3)	15 < 19	30
(4)	19 < 30	34
(5)	30 and over	34

A complete list of the towns, in alphabetical order, is given in the table
in Appendix A. It is worth noting that the smallest towns included e.g.
Canterbury, Hereford, and Salisbury had a population of approximately
30, 000 and total retail sales in 1961 of at least £10 million. The resul
of the analysis might have to be modified when it is extended to take
account of towns of much smaller size.

Limitations of the Analysis

Apart from the limitations just mentioned with regard to the range of
town-sizes included, there are other limitations to the analysis which
need to be mentioned before turning to the results.

16

First, apart from the question of part-time employment, no account has been taken of differences between towns in the structure of the workforce in retailing. In particular, no direct account has been taken of the relative importance of self-employed workers, of the age and sex composition of the labour force, and of the educational attainments or degree of training of the labour force. The first of these factors relates mainly to the number of hours worked, the others are all aspects of labour quality. Some <u>indirect</u> account has been taken of the relative importance between towns, of the numbers of self-employed because we distinguish between 'independents' and 'multiples and co-operatives', and the relative importance of self-employed workers will vary directly with the relative importance of 'independent' shops.

Secondly, it would have been desirable to base an analysis of productivity on other factors of production in addition to labour. In the case of retailing in particular it would have been useful to compare towns on the basis of the ratio of turnover to stocks, since the latter form an important part of the capital of this sector of the economy. Data on stocks are not given, however, on a town basis. But even when this sort of qualification has been taken into account, there is still a great deal of interest in estimates of output per person engaged. In a period of labour shortage, efficiency in the use of labour is important in itself, and, moreover, other productivity studies have generally shown that conclusions based on labour productivity are not greatly changed when other factors of production are taken into account. (1)

Thirdly, the use of sales as an indicator of output is dictated by the fact that it is the only measure available for undertaking a general study of this kind. It is not of course an ideal measure of output. The difficulties are mainly those of the amount of service 'embodied' in the sale of commodities. The types of service involved include such things as the amenities offered to customers, the extent of the aids offered to the customers in the process of buying, the terms of sale, and the range of stocks carried. The problem here is not one of the amount of service 'sold' with a <u>particular</u> commodity but the services associated with a given <u>type of shop</u> within a kind of business. As mentioned above, Britain is a sufficiently homogeneous country to make it reasonable to assume that as between towns of a similar size the product mix and the associated services for any type of shop within a kind of business will be fairly uniform. However there are two difficulties. First, towns differ in the contribution to total sales made by the different kinds of business, and between kinds of business there are differences in the importance of the various types of service. The over-all labour productivity in a town, however, can be adjusted to take account of, say, an unusually high percentage of grocery sales. But there is the second difficulty. Within a kind of business there will be differences in the amount of service associated with the different types of shop, independents for instance as compared to multiples, in the grocery trade. These differences within a

---

) See, for example, W. B. Reddaway and A. D. Smith, Progress in British Manufacturing Industries, 1948-54, <u>Economic Journal</u>, March 1960, p. 29.

kind of business would tend to be reflected in gross margins but are o[n]
partially reflected in the turnover figures because of the importance i[n]
the turnover figures of the cost of goods purchased by the shops. The
problem of services will be raised again during the course of the anal[y]
sis.

Fourthly the sales figures for towns do not include mail order busines[s]
This, however, is an advantage because mail order trade is spread ove[r]
very wide areas and has a very different level of sales per person engaged than other kinds of business. Its inclusion in town totals, theref[c]
might distort the position. (1)

Finally, in distinguishing between kinds of business, sales are broken
down into the seven major kinds of business only:- 'Grocers and Prov[i]
sion Dealers', 'Other Food', 'Confectioners, Tobacconists, Newsagents'
'Clothing and Footwear', 'Household Goods', 'Other Non Food' and
'General Stores'. Some of these, for instance 'General Stores', include[s]
such a variety of shops that we would not expect the analysis to give a[ny]
useful results. (2) Others such as Grocers and Provision Dealers and
Clothing and Footwear are, between towns of a similar size, much mor[e]
uniform in their structure, and it is on these that we will concentrate
most of our attention.

---

(1)   On a national level sales per person engaged in General Mail Or[der]
      business in 1961 (classified under 'General Stores') was £6102
      compared for instance to £3868 for Grocers and Provision Deale[rs]
      and £3100 for all General Stores. See Report on the Census of D[is]
      tribution and Other Services 1961, Part 14, Table 2.

(2)   'General Stores' include Department Stores, Variety Stores and
      Other General Stores—shops selling too wide a range of non-food
      goods to qualify for any of the clothing, household goods or other
      specialist headings.

2. Productivity and Size of Town

retailing a business has a geographically limited market, and the scale of operations depends on the size or density of the local market. is of interest to see, therefore, if productivity varies in any systematic way with size of town. A positive association might be expected on the grounds that larger towns are able to support larger shops which can make fuller use of economies of scale. Of course, there is no <u>necessary</u> association between size of town and size of shop. Larger towns may have <u>more</u> shops rather than larger ones. This is partly a question of the range of town sizes under consideration and partly one of the importance of economies of scale and the degree of competition, the latter determining the extent to which potential economies can be realised. On the question of the range of town sizes, there is clearly some size of town, and 'a fortiori' all smaller sizes, for which economies of scale cannot in general be realised to any important extent. There is also a size of town above which further additions to size do not lead to further significant economies. These critical limits to the size of town will vary from one kind of business to another. The sizes of the smallest towns included in this analysis are probably large enough to allow retail shops most kinds of business to take full advantage of most of the important economies of scale, and the practical applicability of the critical limits the size of town is probably confined to department stores and, to a lesser extent, to clothing shops.

The size of town may be measured by reference to population or to the value of retail sales. Population is an unsatisfactory measure because the average inhabitant of one town may have much more money to spend than his counterpart in another. Moreover the sales of shops in a particular town are not all made to the inhabitants of that town, nor do people living in a particular town purchase all their goods locally: there movement into the town from outside and also an outward movement usually to larger or better shopping centres, and the importance of this migrant custom varies from one town to another. Use of population a measure of town size would mean, therefore, putting towns with very different volumes of retail sales in the same size-class.

The choice of sales then as the indicator of size is determined by the need for uniformity between the towns whose productivity is being compared. The analysis is concerned with the relative efficiency of a town's retailers in carrying out a particular task which is the retailing of a given volume of goods, and the aim of uniformity means putting in the same size-class towns where the volume of goods sold is much the same. (1)

All Retail Trade

The relationship between sales per person engaged (2) and size of town is given in Table 2.1, and it shows a number of striking results.

First, if we look along the average row, we find that labour productivit does not vary significantly with town size but displays quite a remark- able constancy from one size-class to another. The biggest difference between two size-classes is between (4) and (5), sales per person en- gaged being 4 per cent higher in class (4).

In so far as we might have expected a tendency for labour productivity to increase with town size, the observed uniformity might be explained by such a tendency being offset by, for instance, the smaller towns hav

---

(1)   The choice between the two size measures would be of little signi cance if they were closely correlated. In fact there is considerab variability in the relation between total retail sales and population and a further discussion of this relationship is given in the appen- dix to this chapter.

(2)   The figures of sales per person engaged for each town are standa ised, and the reason for this is as follows: As between different kinds of business (grocers, clothing shops etc) the level of sales p person engaged varies quite substantially (see Table 2.5) essenti because the amount of 'service' involved in selling £1,000 worth groceries is much less than the amount for £1,000 worth of clothi This would not matter much if all towns had the same proportion their total retail business in each of the various types of shop, bu does produce a distorting effect on the over-all figures for sales person engaged if one town has, say, a lot of grocery business and another a lot of clothing shops. The object then is to produce a measure of sales per person engaged which would compare towns without being distorted by different proportions of different kinds business. To get the same proportion of sales in the different kin of business for each town in a given size-class we used the avera proportion for the size-class of towns in question. These propor- tions (shown in Table 2.2) were then used to weight the figures fo numbers of persons engaged per £1,000 of sales in each town, and this gave an adjusted figure of persons engaged per £1,000 of sal which was then inverted to give standardised sales per person engaged.

Although the process of adjustment affects the overall sales per person engaged figures for a few towns much more than others, th overall ranking of towns is not greatly changed. The rank correla tions between the ordering of towns in terms of the crude and adjusted data are +0.96, +0.97, +0.95, +0.96 and +0.95 for the size-classes (1) to (5) respectively.

Table 2.1. Sales per Person Engaged (FTE) and Size of Town: in Groups of Towns* All Retail Trade 1961

Town Group	Town Size-Class					Average
	(1)	(2)	(3)	(4)	(5)	
A	4689	4607	4712	4807	4423	4648
B	4402	4390	4321	4479	4165	4351
C	4131	4172	4144	4107	3987	4108
D	3907	3867	3921	3887	3846	3886
E	3654	3560	3690	3682	3678	3653
Average	4157	4119	4158	4192	4020	4129

* The towns in each size class are arranged in descending order of standardised sales per person engaged and divided into groups (A to E) of six or seven.

Source: Census of Distribution and other Services, 1961.

a bigger percentage of retail trade in those kinds of business, such as groceries, which have a high value of sales per person engaged. There is some evidence to support this which is shown in Table 2.2. There is a tendency for the percentage of total retail sales attributable to groceries and provisions, where sales per person engaged are high, to be higher for small towns than for large, the average percentage figure varying from 25 per cent for towns in size-class (1) to 21 per cent in size-class (5). In addition, in General Stores where sales per person engaged are low, there is some tendency for the percentage of retail sales attributable to this kind of business to be higher for large towns than for small ones.

These differences between size-classes, however, are not big enough to offer more than a small part of the explanation of the constancy in labour productivity between size-classes of towns. The more likely explanation is that the towns in the smallest size-class are big enough to enable shops in most kinds of business to take full advantage of the important economies of scale under present conditions of retailing.

The second result shown in Table 2.1 is that the same general uniformity in labour productivity between size-classes is found if we look along the row for any of the Groups A to E. For instance, with the slight exception of class (5), the most 'efficient' group of towns (Group A) in each size-class has much the same level of labour productivity, average sales per person engaged for the five size-classes being £4,648. The 'inefficient' towns in each class have also a very similar performance in terms of labour productivity, with an average sales per person engaged figure of £3,653. At both ends of the productivity scale (i.e. Groups A and E) in no individual size-class does labour productivity vary by more than 5 per cent from the overall average for each Group.

Table 2.2. Average Percentage of Total Retail Sales Attributable to Major Kinds of Business: by Town Size-Class

Kind of Business

Town Size-Class	Groceries and Provisions	Other Food	Confectioner Tobacconists Newsagents	Clothing and Footwear	Household Goods	Other Non Food	General Stores
(1)	25	19	9	16	13	7	11
(2)	25	21	9	15	12	8	10
(3)	22	19	8	18	13	7	13
(4)	22	19	8	19	13	8	11
(5)	21	18	8	17	12	8	16

Source: Census of Distribution and Other Services, 1961

Thirdly, there are big variations in labour productivity between towns within size-classes. Taking an average of the five size-classes, sales per person engaged are 27 per cent higher for towns in Group A than for towns in Group E, and, following from the uniformity noted in the previous paragraph, the difference in labour productivity between Group A and Group E towns is much the same for all size-classes, apart from a smaller difference for class (5). In ascending order of size-class the differences are 28%, 29%, 28%, 31% and 20% respectively.

To summarise, therefore, for all retail trade there is a very high degree of uniformity in labour productivity between size-classes of towns, but there are big variations in labour productivity within size-classes.

Form of Organisation

The pattern of labour productivity, both between size-classes and within them, which was found for all retail trade, is repeated for 'independents' and 'multiples and cooperatives' taken separately. The results are shown in Tables 2.3 and 2.4. For both forms of organisation the differences between size-classes are very small, the most significant depart-

Table 2.3. Sales per Person Engaged (FTE) for Independents: in Groups of Towns

All Retail Trade 1961

| Town Group | Size-Class of Town | | | | | |
	(1)	(2)	(3)	(4)	(5)	Average
A	4065	4083	4022	4101	3985	4051
B	3853	3835	4146	4146	3603	3849
C	3788	3507	3665	3665	3536	3614
D	3479	3475	3388	3388	3454	3430
E	3333	3141	3301	3301	3370	3298
Average	3704	3608	3620	3720	3590	3648

Source· Census of Distribution and Other Services, 1961

ure from the general uniformity being the rather lower figure of sales per person engaged for the largest size-class, particularly for multiples and cooperatives. With a few exceptions, the same general uniformity between size-classes is found for both forms of organisation if we look along the row for any of the Groups A to E.

Table 2.4. Sales per Person Engaged (FTE) for Multiples and Cooperatives: in Groups of Towns

All Retail Trade 1961

Town Group	Size-Class of Town					Average
	(1)	(2)	(3)	(4)	(5)	
A	5521	5276	5369	5415	5028	5322
B	5175	5162	5305	4922	4866	5086
C	4694	4871	4684	4750	4394	4679
D	4377	4419	4690	4441	4314	4448
E	4166	4335	4355	4638	4196	4338
Average	4787	4813	4881	4833	4560	4775

Source: Census of Distribution and Other Services.

Tables 2.3 and 2.4 also show that for both forms of organisation there are big differences in labour productivity within size-classes, and for both, the degree of variation in labour productivity is much the same, with (looking at the average columns) labour productivity of towns in Group A exceeding that of towns in Group E by nearly twenty five per cent in both cases. The absolute level of labour productivity is higher, however, for multiples and cooperatives, with average sales per person engaged for all towns being about one-third higher than for independents—£4775 as compared to £3648.

Kind of Business

In view of the results of the previous sections it is important to take th analysis a little further and to examine the relationship between labour productivity and size of town by kind of business. We are interested pa ticularly in seeing whether the uniformity in labour productivity which has been found between size-classes for all retail trade conceals variations for individual kinds of business. The results are shown in Table 2.5.

In five out of the seven kinds of business (Other Food, Confectioners et Household Goods, Other Non Food and General Stores) there is no tendency for labour productivity either to increase or decrease with size town, and in general the differences in productivity between size-classe are small.

The other two kinds of business (Groceries and Provisions, and Clothin and Footwear) do show some tendency to vary with size of town. For grocers, labour productivity is highest in the smallest size-class and declines as town size increases. Sales per person engaged are £5,500

24

Table 2.5. Average Sales per Person (FTE) Engaged in Town Classes: by Kind of Business

All Retail Trade 1961

Kind of Business	Size-Class of Town				
	(1)	(2)	(3)	(4)	(5)
Groceries and Provisions	5451	5351	5287	5243	5053
Other Food	4279	4178	4211	4235	4087
Confectioners, Tobacconists, Newsagents	4442	4355	4340	4512	4272
Clothing and Footwear	3926	3947	4160	4252	4205
Household Goods	4057	3927	4246	4061	3855
Other Non Foods	3347	3218	3377	3408	3323
General Stores	3228	3444	3368	3454	3340

Source: Census of Distribution and Other Services, 1961.

for size-class (1) compared to £5,100 for size-class (5). For clothing and footwear the relationship between productivity and size of town is reversed with productivity being higher on average for large towns than for small. Sales per person engaged are £4,200 in class (5) as compared to £3,900 in Class (1).

Table 2.6 shows that the relationship between productivity and size of town for these two kinds of business is associated with differences between size-classes in the percentage of sales attributable to multiples and cooperatives.' For grocers, the higher productivity in the smaller size-classes is associated with a higher percentage of sales made by

Table 2.6. Percentage of Sales Attributable to Multiples and Cooperatives: by Kind of Business

Kind of Business	Size-Class of Town				
	(1)	(2)	(3)	(4)	(5)
All Retail	52.5	53.1	53.1	51.7	52.6
Groceries and Provisions*	63.0	61.8	59.1	56.8	55.7
Clothing and Footwear*	57.3	60.2	63.2	62.4	66.8

* Based on information obtained in the 1961 Census of Distribution
ⓒ Board of Trade, 1966

multiples and cooperatives. Compared to size-class (5), sales per person engaged in class (1) are 8 per cent higher and the percentage of sales made by multiples and cooperatives is 13 per cent higher. For clothing and footwear, productivity is highest in the larger towns and so is the percentage of sales attributable to multiples and cooperatives. In size-class (5) sales per person engaged are 7 per cent higher than in class (1) and the percentage of sales made by independents 16 per cent higher. For groceries then both productivity and the percentage of sale attributable to multiples and cooperatives are negatively associated with size of town, and for clothing and footwear both variables are positively associated with town size. How can these relationships be explained?

1. Groceries and Provisions

Part of the explanation for groceries and provisions might well be due to the greater difficulty in large towns than in small in getting into the centre of the town to shop, so that there is a tendency for a smaller percentage of people in large towns to do their shopping in the town centre Since multiples are found mainly in central shopping areas this factor is one which limits their growth and favours the survival of a larger proportion of independents in large towns than in small ones. It is also a factor which we would expect to operate mainly for groceries and provisions, purchases of which are made frequently, and where the cost and inconvenience of getting into the town centre is therefore an important problem. Some evidence to support this argument is shown in Table 2. The percentage of grocery sales made in central shopping areas is a great deal higher in small towns than in large, with an average of 37 per cent for towns in class (1), and 17 per cent for towns in class (5). For

Table 2. 7. Percentage of Sales Made in Central Shopping Areas: by Size-Class of Town

Size-Class of Town	Kind of Business		
	All Retail Trade	Groceries and Provisions	Clothing and Footwear
(1)	51	37	72
(2)	46	34	72
(3)	51	33	77
(4)	47	27	73
(5)	53	17	70
Average	48	30	73

Source: Census of Distribution and Other Services, 1961.

26

clothing and footwear, however, the differences between size-classes in the importance of town centres are much smaller and show no tendency to fall as town size increases. (1)

Secondly, towns in the smallest size-class are big enough for all the economies available in the operation of a branch of a multiple organisation to be realised. But the existence of a multiple branch of given size will have a greater impact on the structure of the retail market in small towns, particularly as in relation to sales, the 'physical' size of towns in size-classes (1) and (2) is often quite small because of the importance of migrant custom. (2)

A third part of the explanation might be that as between towns of very different sizes there is some tendency for the form of competition to differ. It is sometimes argued that whereas the initial competitive impact of multiples is in the form of lower prices, subsequent competition tends to be more in the form of competition in service, especially in the display of a wide range of merchandise. (3) This increases costs by, for instance, increasing space requirements and reducing the ratio of turnover to stocks. We would expect this process to go further in large towns where the competition that a multiple faces comes more from other multiples and less from other types of shop than is the case in smaller towns. In large towns, then, this is a factor enabling independents to maintain a larger share of the market.

2. Clothing and Footwear

Clothing and footwear are 'shopping good', bought more infrequently and for the purchase of which consumers are prepared to travel longer distances than is the case with groceries. Compared to groceries, therefore, we would expect a higher percentage of sales to be made in the central shopping areas where the multiple stores are concentrated, and

---

(1) These figures have to be used with some caution because the 'Central Shopping Areas' do not include subsidiary shopping areas, and the latter increase in importance with town size. How important this point is in modifying the picture given in Table 2. 7 depends on the extent to which multiples are located in the subsidiary shopping areas. The exclusion of the subsidiary shopping areas in the very large towns probably means that the figure shown in Table 2. 7 is a significant underestimate of the 'true' position. If, for example, we exclude the 16 towns with a population of over 250,000, the average percentage of sales made in central shopping is 23 per cent for groceries and 74 per cent for clothing and footwear. The general picture, however, remains unchanged.

(2) This is shown by the fact that whereas the correlation coefficient between grocery sales per inhabitant of the town and <u>sales</u> size of town (for all 160 towns) is —0. 08, for grocery sales per inhabitant and <u>population</u> size of town it is significantly higher at —0. 37.

(3) e.g. P.W.S. Andrews and F. A. Friday. <u>Fair Trade: Resale Price Maintenance Re-examined</u>. p. 56-57.

in fact, taking an average for all size-classes, 73 per cent of clothing and footwear sales were made in town centres compared to 30 per cent for groceries and provisions (Table 2.7.).

There is also some evidence of a positive association between clothing and footwear sales per inhabitant and size of town(1), which is probably mainly due to the importance of migrant custom in these trades.

The higher percentage of sales attributable to multiples and coopera- tives in the larger towns may, therefore, be due to the fact that sales are concentrated in the shopping centres where conditions are suited to mul- tiple store operations, and the fact that, because of the importance of migrant custom which is attracted to the large shopping centres, this process of multiple domination in town centres has gone further in large towns than in small.

Appendix: A Note on Sales per Inhabitant

It was pointed out in Chapter 2 that the choice between population and sales as a measure of the size of town would be of little significance if they were closely related. In fact there is considerable variability in the relation between sales and population size of town, and considerable variation, therefore, in the sales-inhabitant ratio. We look first of all at the variations in the sales-inhabitant ratio within size-classes and attempt to explain why this variation occurs. Secondly, we examine the relation between sales per inhabitant and size of town for all retail trade and for two kinds of business (Groceries, and Clothing and Footwear) taken separately.

1. <u>Sales per inhabitant within size-classes</u>

The full details of sales per inhabitant are given in the tables of Appen- dix B. They show that there are great variations in sales per inhabitant within each size-class. In size-class (1) for instance, the average sales inhabitant ratio is 196, but the highest figure is 361 and the lowest 110. Without taking these extreme values, six towns (i.e. one-fifth of the town in class (1)) have a ratio greater than 250 and six a ratio of less than 145. Even in size-class (5) where the degree of variation is much less than for the other town classes, the variation is still substantial. The average sales-inhabitant ratio is 210 and the extreme values, 293 and 16 Seven towns (one-fifth) have a ratio of over 240, and 7 less than 181.

These variations may be attributed to two main factors:- differences between towns in the level of income per head, and differences in the importance of migrant custom.

(a) <u>Income per head</u>. The relation between sales per inhabitant and income per head is shown in Table 2.6 for the two largest town size- classes. Income per head figures are not available on a town basis and

---

(1) See the appendix to this chapter.

28

the figures shown in the table are obtained by attributing to each town the income per head figure of the county in which it is located. Clearly this is not very satisfactory, and as an indirect measure of income per head we have used the ratio of car licences to households. (1)

Table 2. 8. Sales-Inhabitant Ratios and Income per Head,
in Groups* of Towns
All Retail Trade 1961

| | Town Size-Class | | | | | |
| | (4) | | | (5) | | |
Town Group	Sales per Inhabitant	Income per Head	Car licences/ Households† %	Sales per Inhabitant	Income per Head	Car licences/ Households† %
P	283	719	41. 0	265	724	34. 9
Q	237	706	33. 0	230	715	31. 9
R	206	701	32. 2	206	694	30. 6
S	180	704	24. 7	184	712	31. 5
T	152	710	23. 8	176	707	27. 3

* The towns in each class are arranged in descending order of sales per inhabitant and divided into groups of four or five for class (4) and five or six for class (5).

† Car licences issued by County Borough to residents of the Borough in 1960. Ministry of Transport, Road Motor Vehicles 1962. Number of households from the Census of Population 1960.

There is clearly some tendency for sales per inhabitant to be related to the income per head figures. The table shows that on average the towns with the highest sales-inhabitant ratios are located in the counties with highest-income per head. There is a much better correlation, however, between sales per inhabitant and the ratio of car licences to households, and the range of variation in the latter is also much higher than the income per head figures. Sales per inhabitant in class (4) for example, vary from an average of 283 for towns in Group P to 152 for those in Group T, and the corresponding variation in the ratio of car licences to households is 41 per cent to 24 per cent.

---

(1) It is possible to use this measure for size-classes (4) and (5) where figures of car-licences are available for the majority of towns:- 24 out of 34 in class (4) and 31 out of 34 in class (5). The correlation coefficient between income per head and the ratio of car licences to households is +0. 51 for class (4) and +0. 59 for class (5).

(b) <u>Migrant customs</u>. There are no statistics available on migrant custom but this is obviously an important determinant of the sales-inhabitant ratios of towns. In class (4) for instance, Chester, Exeter, Cambridg
and Oxford—towns with a ratio well above the average for the class—are
all important 'regional' shopping centres. Again there are towns in the
same size-class such as Salford, Oldham and Birkenhead with sales per
inhabitant well below the average, and these are towns which are likely
to have a net loss of customers to larger neighbouring shopping centres.

2. Sales per Inhabitant and Size of Town

Within size-classes then there are big variations in sales per inhabitant
and these are associated with differences between towns in income per
head and in the importance of migrant custom. There is no association,
however, between total retail sales per inhabitant and size of town. In
Table 2.9 both size-class of town and sales per inhabitant groups are
rated (1) to (5). Only 36 out of the 160 towns get the same rating on each

Table 2.9. Cross-Classification of Towns by Sales per Inhabitant and
Sales: 160 Towns, 1961

Sales per inhabitant £	Sales Size-class £m (1) 10 < 12.25	(2) 12.25 < 15	(3) 15 < 19	(4) 19 < 30	(5) 30 and over	Total
(1) Less than 165	13	9	7	5	1	35
(2) 165 < 190	3	4	6	7	13	33
(3) 190 < 225	6	5	4	7	11	33
(4) 225 < 260	4	9	8	9	3	33
(5) 260 and over	5	4	5	6	6	26
Total	31	31	30	34	34	160

Source: Census of Distribution and Other Services, 1961.

test. In other words there is no tendency for the towns to cluster along a
line running from the North-West to the South-East corner of the table.

It is possible of course that although there is no association between
sales per inhabitant and size of town for retail sales as a whole, that
there is an association for individual kinds of business. This possibility
has been examined for Groceries and Provisions and Clothing and Footwear.

For these two kinds of business the data has been presented in the form
of scatter diagrams, each point on the diagrams representing a pair of
values of sales per inhabitant and sales.

30

Diagram 1. Grocers and Provision Dealers: Turnover per Inhabitant and Turnover: 160 Towns, 1961

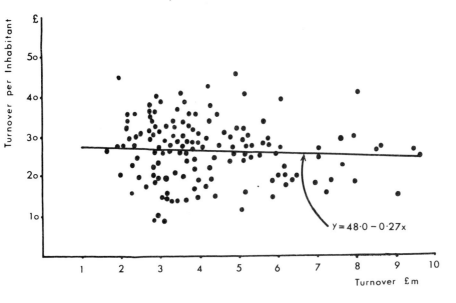

Note: 15 towns have a turnover of more that £10m. and are not included in the diagram.

For Groceries and Provisions there is no clear relationship between sales per inhabitant and sales. The straight line fitted to the diagram, which measures the <u>average</u> relationship between the two variables, shows only a <u>very</u> slight tendency for grocery sales per inhabitant to fall as the volume of grocery sales increases. The line is also a very poor description of the actual data, the actual values of sales per inhabitant often differing very markedly from the ones predicted: the correlation coefficient (r) which measures the strength of the relationship (for perfect correlation all the points would lie on the line and r would equal 1. 0) is very low (0. 21) and if the very large towns are excluded (say the 11 with a population of over 300,000) then the correlation coefficient is virtually nil. (0. 08).

For Clothing and Footwear the association between sales per inhabitant and sales is again a very weak one for all 160 towns. The slope of the straight line (equation Y = 35. 1 + 0. 41x) is very small, showing only a slight tendency for sales per inhabitant to increase with size of towns, and the correlation coefficient is only 0. 14. If, however, we take only those towns with sales of less than, say, £4 million, then there is a much more marked association between sales per inhabitant and sales, shown by the steeper slope of the straight line fitted to the data for these 102 towns. Whereas for all towns an increase in sales of £1 million tends to be associated with an increase in sales per inhabitant of only eight shillings, for the 102 towns with sales of under £4 million, such an increase in sales tends to be associated with an increase in sales per inhabitant of £11. And the correlation coefficient has gone up from 0. 14 to 0. 61.

Diagram 2. Clothing and Footwear; Turnover per Inhabitant and Turnover: 160 Towns, 1961

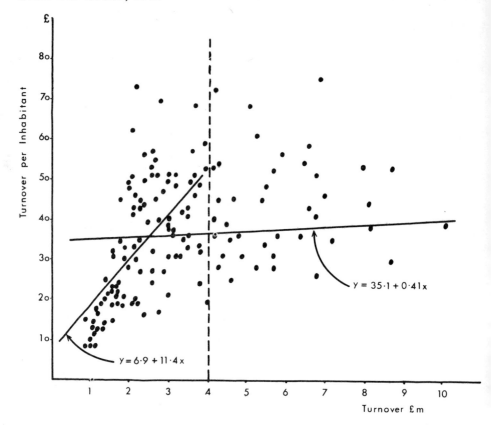

Note: 13 towns have a turnover greater than £10m. and are not included
in the diagram.

To summarise, therefore, for Groceries and Provisions there is no
marked relationship between sales per inhabitant and sales, what associ
ation there is, being a very small negative one and due almost entirely
to the low sales per inhabitant in the very large towns. For Clothing and
Footwear there is a marked positive association between sales per inhabitant and sales for towns with sales up to about £4 million, (1) but the
association is very much weaker for the larger towns.

(1) The population-size of towns with sales of Clothing and Footwear of
     £3.8 m. to £4 m. varies from 68,000 (Chesterfield) to 209,000
     (Harrow).

3 The Structure of Retail Trade

In this chapter we are concerned with the structure of retail trade in towns in the same size-class. The questions to which we attempt to find some sort of answer are looked at under three main headings—'forms of organisation', 'kind of business' and 'central shopping areas'.

Forms of Organisation

With regard to the two major forms of organisation which are distinguished—'independents' and 'multiples and co-operatives'—we look first at the question of whether within each size-class the ranking of towns according to their labour productivity is similar for both forms of organisation. In other words do towns with high over-all productivity have a high level of productivity in both forms of organisation, and similarly for the lower end of the productivity scale. Secondly, again within size-classes, we were interested to see, for individual kinds of business as well as for all retail trade, whether the big variations in labour productivity within size-classes were associated in any systematic way to variations in the percentage of sales made by multiples and co-operatives. (1)

1. The productivity ranking of towns

The full productivity ranking of towns, over-all and by forms of organisation is shown in the tables of Appendix D. A summary of the position is given in Table 3.1.

The first part of the table shows, for each size-class, the average difference between the position of a town in the list of towns ranked according to overall productivity, and its position in the list of towns ranked in terms of the productivity of (a) its independent shops and (b) its multiples and co-operatives. Thus, for instance, Surbiton which is the town with the highest over-all productivity in class (1) also has the highest productivity for multiples and co-operatives taken separately, but is ranked sixth for independents. There is no difference then between its over-all ranking and its ranking in terms of the productivity of its multiple and

---

1) It should be noted that multiples are quantitatively much more important than co-operatives. For instance in the 19 towns in class (4) for which separate information is given for co-operatives, the latter on average accounted for 12 per cent of turnover whereas multiples accounted for 40 per cent.

co-operative stores, but there is a difference of five places, between iț
over-all ranking and its ranking in terms of the productivity of its inde
pendent shops. Table 10 shows the average of these differences for all
the towns in each size-class.

Table 3.1. Difference Between Over-all Productivity Ranking of Towṇ
and Ranking by Productivity in Different Forms of Organisation: by Town Size-Class

| Town Size-Class | Average difference between over-all ranking and ranking for: | | Number of towns with over-all ranking differing by 8 or more places from ranking for: | |
	(a) Independents	(b) Multiples and Co-operatives	(a) Independents	(b) Multiples and Co-operatives
(1)	2.6	2.3	1	1
(2)	3.2	3.8	3	5
(3)	4.0	2.7	6	0
(4)	3.4	5.2	3	10
(5)	3.9	3.9	7	7
Average	3.4	3.6	4	5

Source: Census of Distribution and Other Services, 1961.

The second part of the table shows the number of towns in each size-
class where the difference between the over-all productivity ranking aṇ
the ranking for each form of organisation is eight or more places.

It is clear that, in general, towns with a high level of over-all producti̦
have a high level also in both forms of organisation. Taking the averag̦
for all five size-classes, only three or four places separate the over-a
ranking of a town and its ranking according to the productivity of both ❨
its independent shop and (b) its multiples and co-operatives. Again, onḷ
a small number of towns are ranked very differently by over-all prodụ
tivity performance as compared to productivity in forms of organisatic
taken separately: for independents, on average for all size-classes, onḷ
4 towns out of 32 differ by eight or more places from their over-all
ranking, and for multiples and co-operatives only 5 towns out of 32 diff
to this extent.

With a few exceptions, therefore, towns with a high over-all productivit
have a high level of productivity in both forms of organisation. This is
not surprising, and it suggests that the factors which have affected
labour productivity have been common to all types of shop. One might
expect, for instance, that labour shortage has induced independents as
well as multiples to be more efficient in the use of labour.

Not only is the ranking of towns similar for both forms of organisation
but the amount of variation in productivity in percentage terms is also

much the same. (Table 3. 2). For all size-classes the average percen-age difference between productivity in the top three towns and the bot-om three is 29 per cent for independents and 32 per cent for multiples and co-operatives.

Table 3. 2. Percentage Excess of Average Sales per Person Engaged of Top Three Towns over Bottom Three: by Form of Organisation

Town Size-Class	Independents	Multiples and Co-operatives
(1)	30	39
(2)	36	29
(3)	23	40
(4)	35	25
(5)	20	29
Average	29	32

Source: Census of Distribution and Other Services, 1961.

2. <u>Productivity and the percentage of sales made by multiples and co-operatives</u>

The second question raised above was concerned with what relationship, if any, exists between the big productivity differences which exist within size-classes and the percentage of sales attributable to multiples and co-operatives. We might expect the latter to account for a larger pro-portion of sales in high productivity towns than in low because their labour productivity is higher than that of independent shops. (See Chapter 2 Tables 2. 3., and 2. 4) We look at this relationship first for All Retail Trade and then for Groceries and Clothing and Footwear.

a) <u>All Retail Trade</u>. How far then are the productivity differences within size-classes associated with variations between towns in the percentage of sales made by multiples and co-operatives? In Table 3. 3 these per-centages are given, for each size-class, in groups of towns which are arranged in descending order of labour productivity. There is clearly a general tendency for towns with a high labour productivity to have a high percentage of sales made by multiples and co-operatives compared to low productivity towns. Looking at the average column, the percentage of these sales varies from 59 per cent for towns in Group A to 47 per cent for towns in Group E. The same picture is also found within each indi-vidual size-class.

Table 3. 3. Percentage of Total Retail Sales Attributable to Multiples and Co-operatives: in Groups of Towns*
All Retail Trade, 1961

Town Group	Town Size-Class					Average
	(1)	(2)	(3)	(4)	(5)	
A	57. 9	58. 2	60. 8	62. 7	55. 9	59. 1
B	52. 5	53. 6	50. 5	56. 7	53. 2	53. 3
C	48. 7	57. 0	52. 8	47. 8	53. 7	52. 0
D	54. 8	47. 9	54. 6	49. 8	52. 3	51. 9
E	48. 7	48. 5	46. 8	41. 0	47. 4	46. 5
Average	52. 5	53. 0	53. 1	51. 6	52. 5	52. 5

* The towns in each class are arranged in descending order of standardised sales per person engaged and divided into groups of six or seven.

Source: Census of Distribution and Other Services, 1961.

An alternative way of showing the association between productivity and the proportion of sales made by multiples and co-operatives is to plot the values of the two variables on a scatter diagram, measuring sales per person engaged (the Y variable) on the vertical axis, and the percentage of sales made by multiples and co-operatives (the X variable) on the horizontal axis. This has been done in Diagram 3 for all 160 towns. (1)

There is clearly a positive association between productivity and the importance of multiples and co-operatives in total retail activity, which is shown by a tendency for the points on the diagram to cluster round a line running from the South West corner of the diagram to the North East.

---

(1) It will be remembered that the idea of dividing the 160 towns into 5 size-classes was based on the desirability of maintaining as much uniformity as possible between the towns whose productivity was to be compared. In fact we have found that, for All Retail Trade, there is a very high degree of uniformity between size-classes both in sales per person engaged (see Ch. 2, Table 2. 1) and in the percentage of sales made by multiples and co-operatives (See Table 3. 3). Because of this uniformity it was decided to calculate the regression equation for all 160 towns and give this as the 'average' result rather than calculate the arithmetic average of the results for the five size-classes individually. Had we pursued the latter course the result, however, would have been very similar with a regression equation of $Y = 2785 + 25.56X$, and $r^2 = 0.30$.

36

Diagram 3. Sales per Person Engaged and Percentage Sales Made by Multiples and Co-operatives. 160 Towns 1961

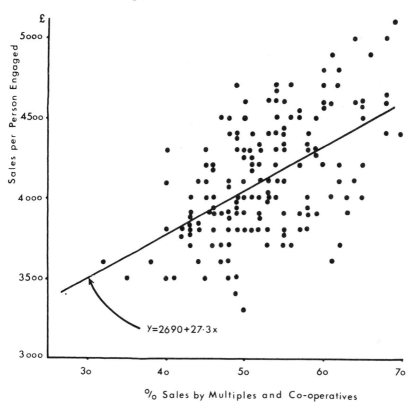

The straight line which has been fitted to the points on the diagram has he equation Y = 2690 + 27. 3X, and it expresses the average relation-hip between Y (labour productivity) and given values of X (percentage ales made by multiples and co-operatives). The above equation tells s that a five per cent increase in the percentage of sales made by mul-iples and co-operatives (say from 40 per cent to 45 per cent) will tend o be associated with an increase in sales per person engaged of about ￡137 (i.e. from ￡3782 to ￡3919).

n addition, the correlation coefficient between the two variables, and lso the square of this coefficient, have been calculated. The latter gives s the degree of statistical explanation, that is, the extent to which vari-tions in labour productivity can be explained statistically by variations n the importance of multiples and co-operatives. (In the case of per-ect correlation all the points representing pairs of values of X and Y ie on a straight line and the correlation coefficient, and its square, is qual to 1. 0 which means that all the variation in one variable can be explained' by reference to movements in the other.) For the data in iagram 3 the square of the correlation coefficient is 0. 30, which means hat 30 per cent of the variations in labour productivity can be 'explained' y reference to variations in the percentage of retail sales made by ultiples and co-operatives.

The regression equations and the correlation coefficients for each size class separately, are shown in Table 3. 4, which contains the regression equations, their standard errors (in brackets) and the squares of the correlation coefficients (r^2). The table shows that in each size-class there is a positive association between the two variables, and in each class the regression coefficients are highly significant. (1)

Table 3. 4. Results of Regression and Correlation Analysis. Sales per Person Engaged (FTE) on Percentage of Total Retail Sales made by Multiples and Co-operatives*

Town Size-Class	Constant	Regression Coefficient	r^2
(1)	3189	18. 15 (9. 60)	0. 11
(2)	2551	29. 30 (8. 60)	0. 29
(3)	2896	23. 76 (7. 69)	0. 25
(4)	2110	40. 41 (16. 17)	0. 71
(5)	3178	16. 17 (7. 10)	0. 14
All Towns†	2690	27. 33 (3. 36)	0. 30

* Based on individual town data.

† Based on individual data for all 160 towns.

What accounts for this association between productivity and the percentage of sales made by multiples and co-operatives?

Part of the explanation is probably due to the fact that multiples have in general concentrated in setting up branches in the most prosperous and rapidly expanding towns. The increased competition resulting from the establishment of multiple stores has the effect of increasing productivity all round. First, the level of productivity in the town is increased by the presence of multiples because of their more capital intensive selling

(1) As an approximate guide, if the value of the regression coefficient is 2. 05 times as great as the standard error it is significantly different from zero at the 5 per cent level. If it is 2. 8 times greater it is significant at the one per cent level. The lower the standard error the greater the level of significance.

techniques which enable important economies in the use of labour to be realised. Secondly, competition from multiples means that some of the inefficient firms are eliminated, which itself increases average productivity in a town, and also that, in order to survive or to maintain market shares, other firms have to reorganise their selling methods on more efficient lines and this will probably mean, amongst other things, higher labour productivity.

Another part of the explanation probably lies in the fact that low productivity towns are often ones where the unemployment rate is relatively high and where the range of job opportunities or, what amounts to much the same thing, long term earnings prospects, are low due to the dominance of the older industries. These labour market conditions might mean a greater incentive to set up (or remain) in business and become (or remain) one's own boss as an alternative to unemployment or blind alley jobs at relatively low wages. These are forces, then, which tend to maintain a bigger proportion of independent shops in low productivity towns.

A third part of the explanation might be that in the older town the pattern of retailing is slower to change. This might be due to the fact that a larger proportion of consumers in the older towns have been slower to change their shopping habits and move their custom in favour of shops using new methods of selling. It might also be due to the greater difficulty, in older towns, for new enterprises to secure suitable vacant sites, or more important perhaps, to the greater cost of converting old buildings into new shops.

Although differences between towns in the relative importance of the two forms of organisation will account for some of the variations in labour productivity these differences are not very important quantitatively in explaining productivity differences. This can be seen by a hypothetical example. In Table 3.5 the second column shows the percentage difference in labour productivity between the top group of towns (Group A) and the bottom group (Group E). The third column shows the percentage differences on the assumption that the percentage of sales made by multiples and co-operatives was the same for each town and equal to the average for the class of towns. This eliminates any 'unfair' advantage a town has in having a low proportion of independents, and the result is to reduce the productivity differences as shown in the last column of Table 3.5. The effect is not very important, the average difference for the five size-classes between the actual and hypothetical productivity differences being only 4 per cent i.e. 29 per cent as compared to 25 per cent.

Although then, multiples account for a bigger proportion of sales in high productivity towns than in low ones, and this accounts for some of the productivity variations within size-classes, far more important is the fact that multiples in high productivity towns have a higher productivity than multiples in low productivity towns, and independents in high productivity towns also have a higher productivity than independents in low productivity towns. This was clearly seen in Table 3.2. which showed that, on average for the five size-classes, productivity in the top three towns exceeded that in the bottom three by 29 per cent for independents and 32

39

Table 3.5. Percentage Difference in Sales per Person
           Engaged between the Top Group of Towns
           and the Bottom Group: by Town Size-Class*

Town Size-Class	Actual	Hypothetical†	Difference
(1)	32	28	—4
(2)	31	27	—4
(3)	27	24	—3
(4)	32	25	—7
(5)	22	20	—2
Average	29	25	—4

Source: Census of Distribution and Other Services, 1961.

* The Table is based on unadjusted sales per person
  engaged figures (Table 2 in the Statistical Appendix)
  because in the 1961 Census of Distribution sales by form
  of organisation are not broken down by kind of business
  for individual towns.

† This column shows the percentage difference in sales
  per person engaged between the top group of towns and
  the bottom group in each size-class, on the assumption
  that the percentage of sales attributable to multiples and
  co-operatives was the same for each town and equal to
  the average for all towns in the size-class.

per cent for multiples and co-operatives. Productivity differences ther
are due mainly to differences within forms of organisation rather than
differences in the proportion of sales made by multiples and co-operatives.

One further point needs to be made about differences in labour productivity as measured by sales per person engaged. Such differences, it
might be argued, exaggerate the difference in real output per person er
gaged because the sales per person engaged figures do not take adequa
account of the greater amount of service embodied in the sale of goods
in independent shops, which account for a large proportion of sales in
low productivity towns. This is certainly a factor to be considered but
too much should not be made of it. The service element associated wit
independent shops normally forms a very small part of turnover and i
one case at least—the range of stocks carried—it might well be that the
element of service involved is greater for multiples. In addition as we
have seen, when the two forms of organisation are looked at separately
the degree of variation in labour productivity is much the same for bot

(b) Groceries and Provisions and Clothing and Footwear. The same
problems of the association within size-classes between productivity a
the proportion of sales made by multiples and co-operatives can be

looked at for individual kinds of business. This we have done for Groceries and Provisions and Clothing and Footwear. The results are shown in Tables 3.6 and 3.7.

Table 3.6. Percentage of Groceries and Provision Sales Attributable to Multiples and Co-operatives: in Groups of Towns*

Town Group	Town Size-Class					
	(1)	(2)	(3)	(4)	(5)	Average
A	75.5	71.0	68.8	74.4	58.5	69.6
B	64.3	67.6	63.2	60.5	55.3	62.8
C	60.0	62.3	56.2	53.8	53.1	57.1
D	57.6	55.4	54.8	49.7	55.6	54.6
E	57.7	52.7	52.5	45.8	52.8	52.3
Average	63.0	61.8	59.1	56.8	55.7	59.3

* Based on information obtained in the 1961 Census of Distribution © Board of Trade, 1966.

Table 3.7. Percentage of Clothing and Footwear Sales Attributable to Multiples and Co-operatives in Groups of Towns*

Town Group	Town Size-Class					
	(1)	(2)	(3)	(4)	(5)	Average
A	48.3	57.1	63.2	67.0	66.8	60.5
B	52.6	67.1	60.8	72.9	67.1	64.1
C	59.8	61.8	64.1	54.0	67.0	61.3
D	68.2	59.2	67.5	60.0	66.9	64.4
E	57.8	55.6	60.4	58.2	66.1	59.6
Average	57.3	60.2	63.2	62.4	66.8	62.0

* Based on information obtained in the 1961 Census of Distribution © Board of Trade, 1966.

For Groceries and Provisions, as for All Retail Trade, there is a positive association between labour productivity and the percentage of sales due to multiples and co-operatives. The latter varies, on average for the five size-classes, from 70 per cent for towns in Group A to 52 per cent for towns in Group E. This is not surprising because the factors mentioned in the previous section to explain this relationship for All Retail Trade—greater competition from multiples in prosperous towns and a

greater incentive to remain in self-employment in towns with relativel
high unemployment—apply more forcibly to groceries than to any other
kind of business.

For Clothing and Footwear, however, there is no significant positive
association between productivity and the proportion of multiple and co-
operative sales, the latter being much the same on average in both high
and low productivity towns (Table 3. 7).

It would appear that, unlike Groceries and Provisions, there has been n
tendency in the Clothing and Footwear trades for multiples to set up
more branches in one set of towns than another. If they had done, one
would expect the attractiveness, in terms of price and range of choice,
of the central shopping areas in such towns to be greater than in others
and, therefore, for a higher percentage of sales to be made in town
centres. This in fact is not the case as shown in Table 3. 8. Whereas i

Table 3. 8. Percentage of Sales Made in Central
Shopping Areas: in Groups of Towns
(Average for Five Size-Classes)

Town Group	Groceries and Provisions	Clothing and Footwear
A	37	76
B	31	67
C	34	74
D	24	80
E	22	70

Source: Census of Distribution and Other
Services, 1961.

groceries the percentage of sales made in central shopping areas does
tend to fall from Group A towns to Group E, there is no such tendency
found for Clothing and Footwear.

Kind of Business

The pattern of variation in labour productivity can be further examined
by distinguishing kinds of business—Groceries and Provisions, Other
Food etc. First we look to see whether the towns which have a high
overall productivity also have a high level of productivity in individual
kinds of business, and similarly for the lower end of the productivity
scale. Secondly we examine by individual kinds of business, the pattern
of productivity variation in the Central Shopping Areas of towns, and
compare the productivity performance in the town centres with performance in the rest of the town.

Table 3.9. Difference Between Overall Productivity Ranking of Towns and Ranking by Productivity in Different Kinds of Business: by Town Size-Class

	Average Movement in Ranking List*						
Town Size-Class	Groceries and Provisions	Other Food	Confectioners Tobacconists Newsagents	Clothing and Footwear	Household Goods	Other Non Food	General Stores
1	3.4	2.3	5.5	9.2	5.5	6.0	9.0
2	4.1	4.3	5.0	6.4	4.5	6.3	8.8
3	4.0	3.9	6.8	6.9	5.3	7.7	6.1
4	3.9	4.1	5.6	4.9	5.4	5.1	11.9
5	6.2	3.4	7.9	6.5	4.5	5.5	7.4
Average	4.4	3.6	6.2	6.8	5.0	6.1	8.6

* The columns show the average difference between the 'over-all' ranking of towns and the ranking list for each kind of business.

Table 3.10. Coefficients of Rank Correlation Between Overall Productivity Ranking of Towns and Ranking by Productivity in Different Kinds of Business: by Town Size-Class

Coefficients of Rank Correlation

Town Size-Class	Groceries and Pro-visions	Other Food	Confectioners Tobacconists Newsagents	Clothing and Footwear	Household Goods	Other Non Food	General Stores
(1)	0.89	0.94	0.73	0.28*	0.71	0.67	0.08*
(2)	0.85	0.80	0.71	0.59	0.81	0.63	0.30*
(3)	0.79	0.85	0.63	0.48*	0.63	0.33*	0.59
(4)	0.87	0.84	0.71	0.77	0.78	0.78	0.01*
(5)	0.66	0.86	0.43	0.59	0.83	0.75	0.50*
Average	0.81	0.86	0.64	0.54	0.75	0.63	0.30*

* Not significantly different from zero at the 5 per cent level.

1. Ranking of towns by kind of business

The extent to which the ranking of towns by each major kind of business conforms to the overall productivity ranking is shown in Table 3.9 and 3.10. Table 3.9 shows, for each size-class, the average difference between the position of a town on the overall ranking list and its position on the ranking list for each kind of business. Table 3.10 gives the coefficients of rank correlation between the overall ranking of towns and their ranking by kind of business. The tables show varying degrees of conformity.

For Groceries and Provisions, Other Food, and Household Goods the ranking of towns conforms reasonably well. The average difference between the overall ranking of a town and its ranking according to the productivity of its shops in these kinds of business is 5 places or less, and the coefficients of rank correlation are, on average for the five size-classes, 0.75 or over. (If all towns had the same ranking on both tests i.e. overall productivity and individual kind of business productivity, the coefficient of rank correlation would be 1.0.) The degree of conformity is significantly less for the remaining kinds of business, and for General Stores it is very low, with an average difference, for all size-classes, between the position of towns in the two ranking lists as high as 9 and a coefficient of rank correlation of only 0.30, which is not significant at the 5 per cent level.

2. Central Shopping Areas

The 1961 Census of Distribution distinguishes Central Shopping Areas (C.S.A.) from the rest of the town. The figures must be treated cautiously because the division between C.S.A.'s and the rest of towns is to some extent an arbitrary one. (1) The figures do, however, seem to form some pattern and there are interesting differences between kinds of business. (2)

We are concerned in this section with the following problems. First, within a town productivity is usually higher in the C.S.A.'s than elsewhere, but are the percentage differences in productivity greater for high productivity towns or for low productivity ones, and is the answer the same for each kind of business? Secondly, are the differences between high and low productivity towns within size-classes greater or smaller in C.S.A.'s than elsewhere? The general picture is given in Tables 3.11 and 3.12 and the main results may be summarised as follows.

a) Groceries and Provisions. For Groceries and Provisions Table 3.11 shows that the difference in sales per person engaged between C.S.A.'s

1) See Report on the Census of Distribution and Other Services 1961, Part 2 p. 6.

2) This section does not include 'Other Non Food' and 'General Stores' because for a large number of towns separate figures are not given for the Central Shopping Areas.

Table 3.11. Percentage Difference in Sales per Person Engaged between Central Shopping Areas and Rest of Town: by Kind of Business. 1961

Kind of Business	Town Group*	Town Size-Class					Average
		(1)	(2)	(3)	(4)	(5)	
i Groceries and	A_i	28	24	24	24	26	25
Provisions	C_i	14	40	18	17	18	21
	E_i	5	7	7	5	8	6
ii Other	A_{ii}	−5	−1	14	4	10	4
	C_{ii}	30	11	10	20	18	18
	E_{ii}	−3	11	18	26	11	13
iii Confectioners	A_{iii}	12	12	40	30	35	26
Tobacconists	C_{iii}	57	69	34	54	36	50
Newsagents	E_{iii}	57	72	53	71	65	64
iv Clothing and	A_{iv}	51	69	70	70	78	68
Footwear	C_{iv}	47	51	46	66	53	53
	E_{iv}	20	49	40	56	40	41
v Household	A_v	25	26	25	40	38	31
Goods	C_v	31	30	32	38	23	31
	E_v	24	37	28	31	16	27

* The towns in each class are arranged in descending order of sales per person engaged in individual kinds of business and divided into groups of six or seven. Thus, Ai is the group containing the six towns with the highest labour productivity in Grocers and Provisions shops, and so on. Groups B and D have been omitted to reduced the size of the table but this does not affect the results given in the text.

Source: Census of Distribution and Other Services, 1961.

and the 'Rest' of towns tends to be greatest, on average, for high productivity towns and the difference declines greatly as we move down the productivity ranking from Group A_i to Group E_i—from an average, for all size-classes, of 25 per cent for towns in Group A_i to 6 per cent for towns in Group E_i. Table 3.12 shows that the degree of superiority of high productivity towns over low productivity ones is greater in the C.S.A.'s—the average difference for all size-classes being 54 per cent in the C.S.A.'s and 30 per cent in the 'Rest'—but even outside the C.S.A. the productivity differences are decidedly big.

This pattern is, in part, a reflection of the fact that multiples have tende to establish more branches in the town centres of prosperous towns. As a result the differences in labour productivity between the C.S.A.'s and the 'Rest' would tend to be greater in these towns, and also, in comparin high and low productivity towns we would expect the difference in labour productivity to be greater in the C.S.A.'s. As mentioned above, however the differences in productivity outside the C.S.A.'s are still big. This is

Table 3.12.   Percentage Difference in Sales per Person Engaged between High and Low Productivity Towns: Central Shopping Areas and Rest of Town. By Kind of Business. 1961

Kind of Business	Town† Group	Town Size-Class* (1) C.S.A.	(1) Rest	(3) C.S.A.	(3) Rest	(5) C.S.A.	(5) Rest	Average (all size-classes) C.S.A.	Average (all size-classes) Rest
Grocers and Provisions	A_i	7271	5747	7152	5794	6899	5539	7188	5774
	E_i	4725	4597	4669	4383	4759	4434	4666	4434
	% Diff.	54	25	53	32	45	25	54	30
Other Food	A_{ii}	5013	5273	5440	4798	5250	4778	5199	5012
	E_{ii}	3133	3336	3867	3306	3716	3288	3719	3317
	% Diff.	60	58	41	45	41	45	40	51
Confectioners Tobacconists Newsagents	A_{iii}	5917	5269	7129	5167	6645	4934	6482	5209
	E_{iii}	4710	3030	4650	3089	5319	3496	5080	3192
	% Diff.	26	73	53	67	25	41	28	63
Clothing and Footwear	A_{iv}	5032	3379	5613	3342	5591	3151	5466	3309
	E_{iv}	3520	3056	4057	2944	4324	3124	3944	2868
	% Diff.	43	11	38	14	29	1	39	15
Household Goods	A_v	4943	4027	5080	4402	4996	3669	5088	3986
	E_v	3809	3145	4024	3112	3649	3149	3824	3047
	% Diff.	30	28	26	42	37	17	33	31

* Size-Classes (2) and (4) are not included but the patterns of productivity variation are similar to those in the size-classes shown.

† The Town Groups A_i and E_i etc. are the highest and lowest productivity groups respectively by kind of business productivity.

Source: Census of Distribution and Other Services, 1961.

consistent with the hypothesis that the greater competition and the high levels of efficiency among grocery shops in town centres forces up efficiency in grocery shops elsewhere. In the present context this suggests that the greater the degree of competition and the higher the level of efficiency in town centres, the greater are the tendencies leading to the more efficient use of resources in shops outside the central shopping areas.

(b) Clothing and Footwear and Household Goods. The same general patterns as are found in Groceries and Provisions are found also in Clothing and Footwear and, but to a much lesser extent, in Household Goods. As in Groceries the superiority of C.S.A.'s over the Rest is greatest in the most productive towns. For Clothing and Footwear the average percentage productivity difference between C.S.A.'s and the 'Rest' for all size-classes is 68 per cent for towns in Group A and 41 per cent for towns in Group E; for Household Goods the figures are 31 per cent and 27 per cent, respectively. (Table 3.11 average column.) And again as in Groceries, the percentage differences in labour productivity between high and low productivity towns is greater in the C.S.A.'s than elsewhere; 39 per cent as compared to 15 per cent for Clothing and Footwear, and 33 per cent as compared to 31 per cent for Household Goods. (Table 3.12 average column.)

But there are some important dissimilarities as well. First, whereas in Groceries and Provisions the productivity differences between the C.S. and the 'Rest' are very small in the low productivity towns (6 per cent on average for the five size-classes, see Table 3.11), in Clothing and Footwear and Household Goods these productivity differences are big in all groups of towns although not as big in the low productivity towns as in the high productivity ones, but even for the low productivity towns (Group E) the difference is 41 per cent for Clothing and Footwear and 27 per cent for Household Goods. (Table 3.11).

The size of the productivity differences between the C.S.A. and the 'Rest' in these kinds of business is in fact much bigger for all groups of towns than it is for Groceries and Provisions. This applies particularly to Clothing and Footwear where the difference in Group A towns for instance is, on average, 68 per cent as compared to 25 per cent for Groceries. It reflects the fact that Clothing and Footwear are 'shopping' goods, the sales of which tend to be highly concentrated in the central shopping areas, so that as compared to grocery shops the advantages of a central location are, relatively to sites elsewhere, much more important.

Secondly, for Household Goods the general pattern of productivity variations referred to above applies markedly only to the two largest size-classes of towns. The fact that, in general, the pattern of productivity differences in Household Goods is not very marked might, in part, reflect the fact that a big section of this trade has been covered by resale price maintenance. This has discouraged the introduction of new, labour saving, methods of selling, the success of which depends largely on being able to offer lower prices than other competitors so as to secure a sufficiently large turnover.

48

c) Confectioners, Tobacconists, Newsagents, and 'Other Food'. For 'Confectioners, Tobacconists, Newsagents' the pattern of productivity variation is the reverse to that found for the preceding kinds of business.

Table 3.11 shows that the superiority of the C.S.A.'s over the 'Rest' is greatest in the low productivity towns; looking at the average column in the Table, the percentage productivity difference is seen to be 26 per cent for towns in Group A and 64 per cent for towns in Group E.

Table 3.12 shows that the superiority of high productivity towns over low productivity ones is greatest outside the C.S.A.'s, but even within the C.S.A.'s the productivity differences are big. Thus looking at the average column, the productivity difference between towns in Groups A and E is 63 per cent outside the C.S.A.'s and 28 per cent inside them.

This pattern of productivity variation is associated with the fact that the bulk of sales in this kind of business is made outside the C.S.A.'s. In towns in size-class (4), for example, 77 per cent of sales is accounted for by the 'Rest' of the town. In consequence, most of the important differences in structure and selling methods which affect productivity are also likely to be found away from the town centres.

Two factors help to explain the low percentage of sales made in town centres. First, there are the low gross margins in this kind of business, which make it difficult to survive in the C.S.A.'s where occupancy costs are high. As between towns this probably forces on shops in the centres a greater degree of uniformity in efficiency, including efficiency in the use of labour, than would be expected outside the shopping centres. Secondly, the other factors influencing location are also different than for groceries and clothing, there being a greater advantage in being near to where people live. This might be thought of as the outcome of the balance between economies of scale and the cost of reaching customers, a balance where a change towards larger size has probably been hindered by the importance of resale price maintenance in this kind of business.

For 'Other Food' the general pattern is similar to that for Confectioners, etc., but the differences between the C.S.A.'s and the 'Rest' of towns are not very marked. The productivity differences between high and low productivity towns for instance are big both within C.S.A.'s and elsewhere. Indeed, as compared to other kinds of business the most striking feature about 'Other Food' is the uniformity in sales per person engaged between C.S.A.'s and the 'Rest' in the high productivity towns. (Table 3.12).

4   The Use of Part-Time Labour

An important feature of employment in retailing is the extensive use of part-time labour. We look first of all at a number of 'structural' features of the part-time labour force such as the proportion of the total workforce which is made up of part-time labour, and whether this proportion varies between establishments of different sizes and between different forms of organisation; the importance of 'Saturday-only' workers who are employed specifically to cope with peak demand; and the numbers of hours worked. We are also interested to see whether the use of part-time labour is related to the degree of tightness in the labour market, and whether it helps to raise productivity.

The part-time labour force

This section is based on the results of a 'Pilot Enquiry into Earnings and Hours of Selling Staff in Retail Distribution' carried out by the Ministry of Labour in May 1965. (1) The results are tentative, but nevertheless of some interest, and they are presented here under two headings—'part-time workers as a percentage of selling-staff', and, 'the number of hours worked'.

1. Part-time workers as a percentage of selling-staff

Of the total selling staff covered by the Enquiry, about 31% were part-time workers. The latter are of two main types: those who work on all or most days of the week but only for part of the day (e.g. afternoon only) and those, mainly 'Saturday-only' workers who are employed specifically to cope with peak demand. Thirteen per cent of the total selling staff were 'Saturday-only' workers. The vast majority of part-time workers (excluding 'Saturday-only') were women 21 and over and they accounted for approximately 94% of this category of the part-time workforce. The 'Saturday-only' workers were made up largely of boys and girls under 18, who accounted for over 70% of this category of the workforce in co-operatives and multiples and nearly 60% in 'Other' organisations.

---

(1) Selling staff include managers, supervisors, shop assistants, store warehouse staff and shop cashiers, but excludes working proprietors and relatives not receiving a definite wage, transport and delivery workers, central warehouse workers. For a fuller description see Ministry of Labour Gazette, December 1965, p. 528.

Table 4.1. Part-time Workers as a Percentage of Total Selling Staff: by Size of Establishment and Form of Organisation. May 1965

	Employee Size of Establishment											
Form of Organization	11-24			25-99			100 & over			Average		
	P.T.	S.O.	Total	P.T.	S.O.	Total	P.T.	S.O.	Total	P.T.	S.O.	Total
Co-operatives	14.3	3.6	17.9	14.9	6.4	21.3	19.3	9.7	29.0	17.5	8.0	25.5
Multiples*	19.8	11.3	31.1	15.0	17.1	32.1	17.7	20.0	37.7	17.4	19.3	36.7
Other	21.7	5.6	27.3	15.0	5.3	20.3	17.8	7.2	25.0	17.7	6.9	24.6
Average	18.8	7.0	25.8	15.0	11.2	26.2	17.9	14.6	32.5	17.8	13.5	31.3

P.T. = all part-time workers excluding Saturday-only workers.

S.O. = Saturday-only workers.

* = Organisation having ten or more branches.

Source: Ministry of Labour Gazette, December 1965. The figures for the size-group '5-10 employees' were not published because it was thought that the sample for this size group was not sufficiently representative.

Table 4.1 shows the importance of part-time workers by size of establishment and form of organisation. The general picture given by the Table may be summarised as follows:

First, looking at the average row (total figures), the percentage of the selling staff which is made up of part-time workers is bigger in large establishments than in small, an average of 33% of the selling-staff bein part-time in establishments with 100 or more employees as against 26% in establishments with 11-24 employees.

Secondly, again looking at the average row, this positive association between the importance of part-time working and size of establishment, is due entirely to 'Saturday-only' workers. As a percentage of the selli staff, 'Saturday-only' workers are twice as important in large establish ments (100 or more employees) as in small ones (11-24 employees).

Thirdly, looking now at the average column ('Total' figures) the percentage of part-time workers is significantly higher in multiples than in other forms of organisation, the total part-time staff accounting for 37% of all selling staff in multiples as compared to about 25% in co-operativ and 'Other' organisations.

Fourthly, again looking at the average columns, this relationship betwee part-time working and form of organisation, is again due entirely to the much greater importance in multiples of 'Saturday-only' workers. On average they account for about one-fifth (19.3%) of the selling staff in multiples, and less than one-tenth of the selling staff in co-operatives and 'Other' organisations.

The most striking feature of Table 4.1 then, is the fact that 'Saturday-only' workers are more important in large establishments than in smal and more important in multiples than in other forms of organisation. For large multiple establishments they account for 20% of the selling staff.

The importance of 'Saturday-only' workers in multiple stores (especial 'large' multiple stores) is not surprising, because these stores are the ones most affected by the Saturday peak demand.

2. Hours worked

The average number of hours worked by part-time employees shows a high degree of uniformity both by size of establishment and by form of organisation. (Table 4.2). In general, part-time workers, excluding 'Saturday-only', work about 24 hours a week and 'Saturday-only' about 8 hours.

Hours worked by part-time employees as a percentage of the full-time working week are shown in Table 4.3. The percentage is substantially lower for multiples than for other forms of organisation, and for multiples it would appear to be nearer the mark in general to count three part-time workers (rather than the conventional two) as equivalent to o full-time worker, whereas for co-operatives and 'Other' the convention assumption is not far out. The lower average hours worked by part-tim employees in multiples is due of course to the greater importance in th form of organisation, of Saturday-only workers.

Table 4.2 Average Weekly Hours of Part-time Workers:
by Size of Establishment and of Organisation.
May 1965

	Employee Size of Establishment		
Form of Organisation	11-24	25-99	100 & Over
(i) Part-time Workers excluding 'Saturday-only'			
Co-operatives	23.9	24.1	23.6
Multiples	23.8	23.8	22.4
Other	23.7	23.2	23.0
(ii) Saturday Only			
Co-operatives	7.3	7.3	7.8
Multiples	7.6	7.6	7.5
Other	7.2	7.2	6.8

Source: Ministry of Labour Gazette, December 1965.

Table 4.3. Average Weekly Hours of Part-time Workers (including
Saturday only) as Percentage of Full-time. By size of
Establishment and Form of Organisation. May 1965

	Employee Size of Establishment		
Form of Organisation	11-24	25-99	100 & over
Co-operatives	49	46	44
Multiples	44	37	37
Other	49	48	46
Number of employees	8,921	27,332	151,847

Source: Ministry of Labour Gazette, December 1965.

For all the establishments included in Table 4.3, the weighted average weekly hours of all part time workers as a percentage of full-time is approximately 40%, which is about half-way between assuming that two part-time workers are equivalent to one full-time worker, and assuming that three part-time workers are so equivalent.

Part-time Labour and the State of the Labour Market

We turn now to the relation between the use of part-time labour and the general state of the labour market. (1) We are concerned particularly w the question of whether part-time labour is used more in towns where labour is scarce than where it is fairly easily obtainable.

Diagram 4. Percentage Part-time Workers 1961 and State of the Labour Market 1957-61. All Retail Trade in 160 Towns

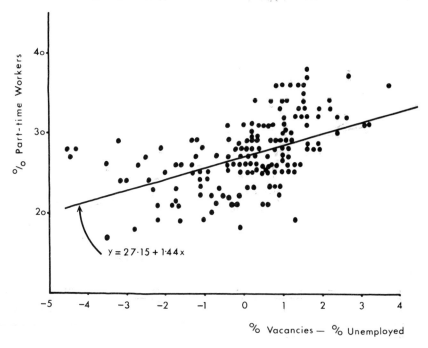

The general picture is shown in Diagram 4. The percentage of the worl force employed on a part time basis varies, taking the extreme cases, between 17% and 38%. Sixteen towns (10%) have a percentage of part-ti workers of 34% or more, and sixteen a percentage of 21 or less. For variations in the degree of tightness in the labour market, as measured

---

(1) The degree of tightness in the labour market is measured by percentage vacancies minus percentage unemployed, and an average measure for the period 1957 to 1961 has been taken. The reason fc this is given on p. 60.

percentage vacencies minus percentage unemployed, the extreme cases are —6.8% and +3.7%. For 16 towns this measure is —2.2% or over, and for 16 it is +1.7% or over.

The diagram also shows that there is some tendency for towns with the highest percentage of the workforce employed on a part-time basis to have the greatest degree of tightness in the labour market. The average relationship between the two variables is given by the straight line which has been fitted to the diagram. This line has the equation $Y = 27.15 + 1.44X$ which tells us that an increase of 1% in % vacancies minus % unemployed (say from 0 to 1) will tend to be associated with an increase of 1.4 per cent in the percentage of the workforce engaged on a part-time basis (i.e. from 27 per cent to 28.4 per cent). However, this is only a rough tendency. Many points on the diagram lie well away from the line so that for a number of towns the actual percentage of part-time workers associated with the given labour market conditions will be very different from the one predicted by the equation.

Table 4.4. Regression and Correlation Analysis.
Use of Part-time Labour on State of the Labour Market.*
All Retail Trade

Town Size Class	Constant	Regression Coefficient (Standard error)	r^2
(1)	27.84	1.84 (0.47)	0.35
(2)	26.14	0.90 (0.45)	0.12
(3)	27.85	1.38 (0.41)	0.29
(4)	26.74	1.70 (0.43)	0.33
(5)	27.02	1.39 (0.44)	0.24
All Towns†	27.15	1.44 (0.19)	0.26

* Based on individual town data.
† See footnote on p. 54.

For all 160 towns the square of the correlation coefficient is 0.26, which tells us that about one-quarter of the variation in the use of part-time labour can be explained statistically by reference to variations in the degree of tightness in the labour market.

The results of the regression and correlation analysis for the towns in each size-class separately, are given in Table 4.4, which shows the regression coefficients, their standard errors (in brackets) and the r^2s. The results are all highly significant.

The evidence is consistent, therefore with the hypothesis that the use of part-time labour is positively related to the degree of scarcity of labour, but variations in the degree of over-all tightness in the labour market offers only a partial explanation of variations in the percentage of the workforce employed on a part-time basis.

Part-time labour and productivity

Is there any systematic association between the use of part-time labour and output per head? The general picture is given in Tables 4.5 and 4.

Firstly, comparing size-classes, there is a great deal of uniformity in the percentage of the workforce employed on a part-time basis. The average figure for all size-classes is 27 per cent, and the figures for each individual size-class vary by no more than one percentage point of either side of this.

Table 4.5. Part-time Workers as a Percentage of
Total Engaged in Groups of Towns

Town Group	Town Size-Class					Average
	(1)	(2)	(3)	(4)	(5)	
A	34	30	33	31	31	31
B	31	30	30	28	26	29
C	28	23	27	27	25	26
D	27	26	25	25	25	26
E	23	24	26	27	25	25
Average	28	26	28	28	26	27

Source: Census of Distribution and Other Services, 1961.

Secondly, table 4.5 shows a clear tendency for the towns with a high level of labour productivity (in Groups A and B) to have a higher percentage of their workforce engaged on a part-time basis than the low productivity towns in Group D and E. On average for the five size-classes, the percentage of the workforce made up of part-time workers varies from 31 per cent for the towns at the top end of the productivity scale to 25 per cent for those at the bottom. Looking at the size-classes individually there is again a great deal of uniformity at both ends of the productivity scale, with employment of part-time workers accounting for between 30 per cent and 34 per cent of persons engaged in Group A towns, and for between 23 per cent and 27 per cent of persons engaged in Group E towns.

Table 4.6 gives for each size-class individually and for all towns together the regression equations and the squares of the correlation coefficients. The regression coefficients are all highly significant. For

56

Table 4.6.   Results of Regression and Correlation Analysis: Sales
Sales per Person Engaged on Use of Part-time Labour.*
All Retail Trade 1961

Town Size-Class	Constant	Regression Coefficient (standard error)	r^2
(1)	2732	49.72 (8.63)	0.53
(2)	3065	39.57 (14.57)	0.20
(3)	2489	59.25 (13.30)	0.41
(4)	2695	54.65 (17.29)	0.24
(5)	3116	34.75 (10.52)	0.25
All Towns	2831	47.45 (5.49)	0.32

* Based on individual town data.

'All Towns' the regression equation, $Y = 2831 + 47.5X$, tells us that a one per cent increase in the percentage of the labour force made up of part-time workers (say from 26 per cent to 27 per cent) will tend to be associated with an increase of £47 in sales per person engaged. And the square of the correlation coefficient, 0.32, tells us that about one-third of the variations in sales per person engaged can be 'explained' by reference to the variations in the percentage importance of part-time labour.(1)

The greater proportion of the employment of part-time labour, however, occurs independently of variations in the state of the labour market.

_____

(1)   Because high productivity towns tend to have a high percentage of part-time labour, and because the conventional assumption of counting two part-time workers as equivalent to one full-time worker overestimates the hours worked part time, the productivity difference between high and low productivity towns is underestimated. We saw above, p. 54, that the average weekly hours of part-time workers as a percentage of the full working week was about 40%. The effect, however, on inter town productivity differences, in counting $2\frac{1}{2}$ part-time workers (instead of 2) as equivalent to one full-time, is small. On average, for the five size-classes, the affect is to increase the percentage difference in the labour productivity of the top group of towns over the bottom group from 27 per cent to 28.5 per cent.

Approximately 25 per cent of the workforce are employed part-time
even in the lowest productivity group of towns where the shortage of
labour tends to be least acute. This is not difficult to explain. A featur
of retail trade in all towns is the existence of marked peaks in demand
which makes it profitable for shops in all towns to employ part-time
rather than full time labour at certain times of the week. This obvious
applies to the Saturday peak but it also applies to the employment of
part-time labour at busy times of the day in mid-week.

Although a high proportion of part-time labour is common to all towns,
high productivity towns nevertheless have a somewhat higher proportio
of part-time labour than low productivity ones, as shown above. This
can be explained in a number of ways.

First, there is the fact that high productivity towns tend to be ones with
the greatest degree of labour shortage, and it was seen in the previous
section that towns with tight labour market conditions tend to employ a
larger percentage of workers on a part-time basis. There is a greater
incentive to employ part-time labour in these towns because of the greater
difficulty in getting full-time staff. But even if some full-time workers
were available their quality might be so low that it would still pay
management to engage part-time workers instead.

Secondly, the use of part-time labour is affected by the extent to which
management has considered the problem of peak demand and the cost o
alternative ways of meeting it. There is 'evidence that by the careful
planning of hours for part-time employees a considerable increase in
productivity is possible'. (1) At the same time, however, problems of
management may be increased by having to employ part-time labour, s
that whereas, with given methods of selling, productivity can be increa
by such employment, there may well be a tendency in the longer run to
change to new selling methods which are less dependent on part-time
labour. It is interesting to note, for instance, that the 1961 Census info
mation on self service grocery stores shows that they were less depen
dent on part-time staff than counter service shops. Less than one in fi
self service staff were employed part-time as against more than one i
four in other grocery shops.

Thirdly, variations in the use of part-time labour will also occur as a
result of the varying importance of different forms of organisation. Ar
example of this is the greater importance in some towns, especially in
the North, of co-operatives, which employ much less part-time labour
than other forms of organisation.

The greater importance of part-time workers in high productivity town
is, therefore, the outcome of a combination of labour market, manageri
and structural forces.

---

(1) Malcolm P. McNair. Explorations in Retailing, Stanley C. Hollande
     Michigan State University, 1959.

5   An Explanation of Productivity Differences

In this chapter we examine the extent to which a combination of factors gives a statistical explanation of sales per person engaged. We start by examining the hypothesis that labour productivity (as measured by sales per person engaged) is significantly affected by the degree of tightness in the labour market. Having found the extent to which variations in the state of the labour market offer an "explanation" of differences in productivity we then go on to see how far the explanation is improved by introducing other explanatory variables. Thus we introduce the size of shop, the market share of multiples and co-operatives and income per head and examine, first, the extent to which each of these variables by itself can "explain" differences in productivity, and second what the over-all degree of explanation is by including all variables in a multiple regression analysis.

The above relates to retail trade as a whole. We are also interested to see the extent to which the same kind of analysis can explain variations in labour productivity in individual kinds of business, and to compare the apparent importance of (for example) labour shortage as an explanatory factor for groceries and for clothing and footwear.

Before going on to the main part of the analysis it is necessary to make the following points.

First, in interpreting the results of the regression analysis we will concentrate on the regression equation for all 160 towns taken together, although several tables will also include the results for each size-class taken separately. We have mentioned several times in this Paper that in many respects there is a great deal of uniformity between size-classes. This is, in general, confirmed by the regression analysis which suggests that, in respect of the data which we are considering, all the towns are taken from the same "population", and the relationship between variables such as sales per person engaged and the state of the labour market, are in general best explained by a line of "best" fit which is fitted to all 160 pairs of observations. In the results this is reflected by the fact that for all 160 towns taken together the standard errors of the regression coefficients are a lot lower than they are for any of the five size-classes taken separately.

Secondly, the interpretation of the results of the regression analysis is complicated by the fact that the factors we use to "explain" labour productivity are themselves correlated. The degrees of inter-correlation between pairs of explanatory variables are shown in Table 5.1. The existence of a positive correlation between the labour market and income per head variables, for instance, means that if a positive correlation is found to exist between labour productivity and income per head, this may be due in part to the fact that both are correlated to the degree of tightness in the labour market. Similarly the existence of inter-correlations introduces some degree of ambiguity into the interpretation of multiple regresssion equation (i.e. equations which include more than on explanatory variable.)

Table 5. 1.

Variables	r^{2*}
L and % M ϵ C	0.06
L and S/S	0.20
L and Y/H	0.42
%M ϵ C and S/S	0.37
%M ϵ C and Y/H	0.05
S/S and Y/H	0.12

* all values of r are positive.

L = % vacancies minus % unemployed, average 1957-1961.

% M ϵ C = market share of multiples and co-operatives.

S/S = sales per shop.

Y/H = income per head.

All Retail Trade

1. The state of the labour market

There are marked differences as between the towns in this study in the state of the labour market.(1) The general picture was given in Chapter where it was shown that, taking the extreme values, the excess of percen tage vacancies over the percentage of unemployment varies from +3. 7 per cent to —6. 8 per cent, and that on a more conservative basis, ten pe

---

(1) The state of the labour market is measured by the average excess of percentage vacancies over the percentage of unemployment for the five year period 1957 to 1961 inclusive. The figures are for Jur in each year. A five year period before the Census was taken as th sort of period over which the longer term adjustments to a labour shortage could be expected to take place. Like all other measures of the degree of tightness in the labour market the one used here is not ideal. It is possible for instance that two towns will show the same excess of percentage vacancies over the percentage of unemployment, but in fact have different labour market conditions. This may be due for instance to differences in the age and sex composition of the workforce, and to differences in the rate of labour turnover.

cent of the towns (i.e. the 16 with the greatest degree of labour shortage) have an excess of percentage vacancies over the percentage of unemployment of 1.6 per cent or more, and for ten per cent (i.e. the 16 with the greatest degree of slack in the labour market) the figure is −2.2 per cent or more.

As far as the distributive trades are concerned one of the most important manifestations of labour market tightness are the abundant job opportunities available in manufacturing industries where weekly earnings are in general higher than for comparable workers in distribution. Where the demand for labour is high and job opportunities are abundant, the distributive trades are likely to find great difficulty in recruiting employees, and in addition there is likely to be a tendency for the existing staff to be able to bargain successfully for higher earnings.

Under such circumstances what labour the distributive trades are able to attract might well be of very low quality and have a high rate of turnover. As to quality, it has been pointed out that 'British retailing recruits fewer people with more than the minimum of schooling, and takes fewer people into apprenticeship or professional training than do other occupations'.(1) As to the high rate of turnover, this may be due partly to the movement of workers into manufacturing industries as suitable vacancies arise in the latter, and partly to the high proportion of female labour employed in retailing.(2) Another factor which probably affects both the average quality of the labour force and the rate of labour turnover is the extensive use of part-time labour. It was seen in Chapter 4 that towns where labour is scarce tend to employ an above average percentage of part-time workers, and that although the employment of part-time workers may well increase labour productivity it may also add to the problems of management.

The greater the scarcity of labour, therefore, the greater is the difficulty in getting full-time staff, the more expensive labour becomes, and the greater tend to be the problems of management as a result of low quality, high turnover rates and greater dependence on part-time labour.

How does a general scarcity of labour affect productivity in the retail trades? The immediate effect might simply be that customers have to wait longer before they are served. In so far as this occurs, although the money value of sales per person engaged will increase, it might be argued that this exaggerates the increase in 'real' output per person engaged because of the reduction in service. In the short run it will usually be possible to relieve the situation by employing more part-time labour at peak demand periods and by introducing some changes in working methods so as to make more efficient use of existing staff.

Over the longer term efficiency in the use of labour can be increased by more substantial changes in working methods, in the lay-out of shops,

---

(1) W. C. McClelland: Studies in Retailing, Oxford, Basil Blackwell, 1963, p. 11.

(2) An average rate of labour turnover of 30 to 40 per cent among female staff in Central London has been mentioned. See Christina Fulop: Competition for Consumers, Andre Deutsch, p. 179.

and by the elimination of unnecessary jobs.(1) In these respects large firms have an advantage over small ones in so far as their larger labour force gives greater flexibility in the use of labour and in so far as they can afford to employ or to consult experts in work-study techniques.

Further saving in labour is made possible by the introduction of entirely new selling methods such as self-service, and self-selection. The raising of labour productivity in retailing is limited by the difficulty in securing continuity in the work of employees due to the existence of marked peaks in demand. The main benefit of self service and self selection is that they have enabled a greater degree of continuity to be achieved by lowering the proportion of employees whose work is dependent on the consumer's presence. The large turnovers associated with these shops also justify the increased use of capital in the form of, for instance, mechanical handling equipment, and for clerical and cash handling operations.

In towns where labour demand conditions are slack and where it is relatively easy for retail firms to get new staff there is less incentive to reorganise selling methods so as to reduce labour requirements. The forces affecting the amount of self-employment are also different. There will tend to be more self employment as an alternative to unemployment or 'dead end' jobs in other industries. In addition the fact that new methods of selling are not so important means that there is less competitive pressure on the inefficient firms so that a larger proportion are able to survive.

Some evidence of the relationship between the state of the labour market and the importance of self service grocery shops is given in Table 5.2. The Table shows that in general, though with important exceptions, the development of self-service has gone further the greater the degree of tightness in the labour market, as measured by the percentage of unemployment. In the London and South Eastern Region, where over 30 per cent of grocery sales in 1961 were made through self-service shops, the development of self-service is reflected in a decline in the number of grocery shops between 1957 and 1961 of approximately 8 per cent. In the Southern and Eastern Regions the development of self service has not been associated with a decline in the number of shops, but as compared to London and the South East the shops in these regions are spread more widely and there has been a much more rapid increase in the size of the market. Using the increase in total retail sales as a rough approximation to the relative rates of growth from 1957 to 1961, the value of sales increased by 16 per cent in the London and South Eastern Region and by about 27 per cent in the Eastern and Southern regions.(2)

The general relationship between labour productivity and the state of the labour market is shown in Table 5.3. The towns are arranged in des-

_____

(1) For examples of the savings that can be made by changes of this sort see for instance Christina Fulop, op.cit. pp. 185-186.

(2) An exact figure is not available for the Southern Region because of a boundary change in 1961.

Table 5.2. Turnover of Self Service Grocery Shops as Percentage of Total Grocery Turnover: by Region

	Turnover as percentage of total, 1961*	Percentage of Workforce Unemployed † (Average 1957-61)
London & South Eastern	31.3	1.1
Southern	28.3	1.3
Eastern	26.9	1.2
Midland	19.8	1.3
North Midland	17.6	1.1
South Western	16.4	1.8
Scotland	16.2	3.3
North Western	15.6	2.2
Northern	14.3	2.5
East & West Ridings	13.2	1.4
Wales	13.0	3.2
Great Britain	20.3	1.7

* Board of Trade Journal, 20th December, 1963
† Ministry of Labour Gazette

Table 5.3. Excess of Percentage Vacancies over Percentage of Unemployment. Average 1957-1961: in Groups of Towns

Town Group*	Town Size-Class					
	(1)	(2)	(3)	(4)	(5)	Average
A	1.4	1.7	1.4	1.6	1.0	1.4
B	1.0	1.0	1.4	1.4	0.1	1.0
C	1.1	—0.1	0.6	0.7	—0.7	0.3
D	0.4	—0.7	—1.2	—0.3	—1.4	—0.6
E	—2.2	—1.3	—1.0	—0.9	—1.7	—1.4

* The towns in each class are arranged in descending order of standardised sales per person engaged and divided into groups of six or seven.

Source: Information obtained directly from the Ministry of Labour

cending order of standardised sales per person engaged (FTE) (1) and
there is clearly a tendency for them also to be arranged in descending
order of degrees of tightness in the labour market. The towns with the
highest productivity, therefore, tend to have the greatest degree of tight
ness in the labour market and those with the lowest productivity have th
greatest degree of slack in the labour market. On average for the five
size-classes, the excess of percentage vacancies over the percentage o
unemployment varies from +1.4 for towns in Group A to −1.4 for those
in Group E.

Table 5.4.   Regression of Sales per Person Engaged
on Excess of Percentage Vacancies over
the Percentage of Unemployment*

Town Size Class	Constant	Regression Coefficient	r^2
(1)	4105	136.40 (30.04)	0.42
(2)	4091	160.93 (29.90)	0.50
(3)	4120	163.85 (32.21)	0.48
(4)	4072	245.99 (39.30)	0.55
(5)	4105	143.31 (23.71)	0.53
All towns	4108	164.25 (13.38)	0.49

* Using data for each town. This table, and others
giving the regression results, contains the regression
coefficients, their standard errors (in brackets) and
the squares of the correlation coefficients (r^2).

The results of the regression of sales per person engaged on the state
the labour market are given in Table 5.4. For all 160 towns the regres
sion equation tells us that a one per cent increase in the excess of per
centage vacancies over the percentage of unemployment (say from 0 to
per cent) will tend to be associated with an increase of £164 in sales
per person engaged. The square of the correlation coefficient is 0.49
which means that about one-half of the variation in labour productivity
can be explained statistically by reference to variations in the degree
tightness in the labour market.

_____

(1)   See footnote on p.20. The entire discussion of labour productivity
with respect to all retail trade refers to standardised sales per
person engaged.

2. The sales size of shop and the percentage of sales made by multiples and co-operatives.

Although the state of the labour market appears to be an important factor in explaining variations in labour productivity the explanation is obviously not complete. We now examine whether labour productivity is significantly related to size of shop and to the market share of multiples and co-operatives.

a) <u>Size of shop</u> The size of shop affects productivity because of the association of size with certain economies of scale. The economics which are most relevant in considering output per head are mainly those related to the imperfect divisibility of labour (including management) and capital.

Large shops, for instance, are likely to be able to adjust the number of their employees more accurately to given levels of demand. The average number of persons engaged per shop in 1961 for all retail trade (a part-time worker counted as one) was only 4.5, and three quarters of all shops employed less than 5 persons. With such small number (and small sales area!) it is clearly very difficult to make accurate adjustments of the labour force to changing levels of demand even allowing for the additional flexibility introduced by the employment of part-time labour. In larger shops this problem of indivisibility in the employment of labour is less and this will lead to higher output per head.

In addition, large shops can take fuller advantage of specialisation in the use of labour. Employees can be given specific tasks to perform which reduces the amount of time wasted in moving from one job to another and which allows shops to make fuller use of the special capabilities of individuals. More important perhaps is the fact that large shops can take advantage of specialisation of management. Whereas in small stores the manager will spend a large proportion of his time serving, in large ones the management can work full time on such problems as how to reduce costs, and some of the measures taken towards this end, such as reorganising methods of work and improving the layout of shops, will increase labour productivity.

Table 5.5. Standardised Sales Size of Shop: in Groups of Towns 1961

£1000

Town Group	Town Size-Class					
	(1)	(2)	(3)	(4)	(5)	Average
A	22.6	21.5	23.1	26.5	22.4	23.2
B	20.1	19.3	19.2	21.0	18.9	19.7
C	19.1	19.6	19.3	18.6	18.8	19.1
D	15.9	15.5	16.8	17.3	19.3	17.0
E	18.0	13.0	15.4	11.5	18.1	15.2

Source: Census of Distribution and other Services, 1961.

Again, large shops will be able to make greater use of capital such as mechanical handling equipment and cash registers which small shops find to be too expensive to employ.

The general relationship between labour productivity and sales size of shop(1) is shown in Table 5.5. The town groups are arranged in descending order of standardised sales per person engaged (FTE) and, on average for the five size-classes, they are also arranged in descending order of standardised sales size of shop, the latter varying from an average of £23,200 for towns in Group A to £15,200 for towns in Group E.

The regression equations of sales per person engaged on sales size of shop are given in Table 5.6. The regression coefficients are all highly

Table 5.6.   Regression of Sales per Person Engaged
             on Sales Size of Shop

Town Size Class	Constant	Regression Coefficient	r^2
(1)	3094	0.054 (0.015)	0.30
(2)	2711	0.079 (0.011)	0.66
(3)	2967	0.063 (0.014)	0.43
(4)	3050	0.060 (0.007)	0.67
(5)	3273	0.039 (0.014)	0.19
(6)	3008	0.059 (0.005)	0.45

* Based on individual town data

(1)   The figures of sales size of shop are 'standardised' figures. The reasons for standardising the figures are similar to those given for standardising sales per person engaged. (See footnote p. 20.) There are firstly, variations between kinds of business in sales per shop, which would not matter much if all towns had the same proportion of sales in each kind of business. But there are also variations between towns in the percentage of sales accounted for by individual kinds of business. To remove these distortions the average percentages of sales in each kind of business for all towns in a size-class were calculated, and these figures were used to weight the figures of shops per £'000 of sales in each kind of business in each town. This gave a standardised figure of shops per £'000 of sales for each town which was inverted to give standardised sales per shop.

66

significant, and for All Towns, the equation tells us that an increase of £1,000 in sales per shop tends to be associated with an increase of £59 in sales per person engaged. The square of the coefficient of correlation is 0.45 which means that 45 per cent of the variation in sales per person engaged can be 'explained' by reference to variations in sales per shop.

(b) <u>The market share of multiples and co-operatives</u> The economies of scale mentioned above are relevant to all large firms whether they are multiples, co-operatives, or independents, and whether the method of selling is self-service, self-selection or counter service. But labour productivity can vary between towns as a result of differences in the percentage of sales made by multiples and co-operatives, which in part, is due to differences in methods of selling. In 1961, average sales per person engaged (counting two part-timers as equivalent to one full-time worker) in self-service grocery shops, for instance, were £6,200 as against less than £4,700 in other grocers. And in the same year, out of a total of approximately £500 million in self-service sales by grocery shops, approximately £440 million (or 88 per cent) was made by multiples and co-operatives. Because of this association of different selling methods with different forms or organisation it is likely that differences between towns in labour productivity are related to differences in the proportion of sales made by multiples and co-operatives.

The general relationship between labour productivity and the market share of multiples and co-operatives has already been examined in Chapter 3, where it was seen that for all 160 towns the regression equation was $y = 2690 + 27.3_x$. This tells us that an increase of ten per cent in the percentage of sales made by multiples and co-operatives (say from 35 per cent to 45 per cent) will tend to be associated with an increase of £273 in sales per person engaged. The degree of 'explanation' of productivity differences was 30 per cent.

3. Income per head

A number of reasons may be suggested as to why labour productivity is likely to be related to income per head. In the first place a high level of income per head is associated with a high level of expenditure per head. This enlarges the size of the market and makes possible an increase in the average size of shop, although it can also be taken out in the form of more shops rather than bigger ones. But secondly, and more important, is the effect which higher income per head has on increasing the size of individual transactions. The latter may take the form of the purchase at one time of more goods of a given quality—either larger units or more units of the same size—or the purchase of higher quality goods, or a wider variety of goods, or some combination of all three. Size of transaction is analagous to the production run in manufacturing where, because of the cost of setting up and closing a run and the delay in changing from one run to another, productivity increases as the length of run increases. Applied to retail shops the argument is that productivity increases as the size of transaction increases. In other words, the smaller the number of customers who account for a given value of retail sales, the less the labour required. This applies particularly where increases in transaction size are in the form of larger quantities of the same goods, but probably also applies, although less forcibly, to situations where larger transactions are due to a wider variety of goods purchased.

The transactions affect is increased by the greater mobility of consumers with high per capita income, and also, in the case of foodstuffs, by better home storage facilities. A greater degree of mobility also reduces market imperfections caused by the distribution of consumers over an area and tends to favour chain stores to the disadvantage of small independent stores.

Further plausibility is given to the argument that income per head is positively related to labour productivity by the hypothesis that there is positive association between income per head and the quality of the labour force (including management). Thus one might expect that the employees in high income towns had received more 'schooling' than those low income ones, and that management in high income towns were also more highly trained and more conscious of the desirability, for instance of encouraging their staff to attend retail training courses.

The general picture showing the relationship between labour productivity and income per head is given in Table 5.7. On average, for the five size

Table 5.7. Income per Head*: in Groups of Towns

Town Group	Town Size-Class					Average
	(1)	(2)	(3)	(4)	(5)	
A	766	756	764	765	765	763
B	748	746	753	742	722	742
C	741	710	706	712	701	714
D	703	699	702	697	685	697
E	688	689	696	706	692	694

* Source: Inland Revenue Report 1960.

classes income per head varies from £763 in towns with the highest sale per person engaged, to £694 in towns at the other end of the productivity scale.

The results of the regression of sales per person engaged on income p head are shown in Table 5.8. The regression coefficients are all highly significant, and for All Towns the equation tells us that on average an i crease of £10 in income per head will be associated with an increase o £73 in sales per person engaged. The degree of explanation is 52 per cent.

These results, however, must be treated with caution. First, as seen in Table 5.1 income per head is quite strongly correlated to the degree o tightness in the labour market. This is in part due to the fact that when labour is scarce, earnings are likely to be high as a result of overtime and various bonus payments negotiated by local bargaining, and this in-

Table 5.8. Regression of Sales per Person Engaged on Income per Head

Town Size-Class	Constant	Regression Coefficient	r^2
(1)	−949	6.99 (1.17)	0.55
(2)	−1839	8.26 (1.48)	0.52
(3)	−1008	7.13 (1.26)	0.53
(4)	−2086	8.68 (1.49)	0.52
(5)	36	5.60 (0.87)	0.56
All Towns	−1170	7.34 (0.56)	0.52

creases income per head. Part of the positive correlation between sales per person engaged and income per head, therefore, may be due to the fact that the latter is correlated with the state of the labour market which in turn is correlated with sales per person engaged. Secondly, and more important, the data on income per head is very unsatisfactory. In the absence of town data we have attributed to each town the income per head figure of the county in which it is located.

For 55 towns in size-classes (4) and (5), however, we have used the ratio of car licences to households as an indirect measure of income per head. The regression of sales per person engaged on this ratio is given by the equation $Y = 3398 + 19.1X$. The regression coefficient is highly signifi- (4.07) cant and tells us that a town with a ratio of car licences to households ten per cent, say, above average (e.g., 41 per cent rather than 31 per cent) will tend to have a sales per person engaged figure £191 above average. The value of r^2 is 0.29, which means that between one quarter and one-third of the variation in sales per person engaged can be 'explained' by variations in the ratio of car licences to households. The degree of 'explanation is much lower than that obtained in size-classes (4) and (5) by the use of county data of income per head, but nevertheless the analysis helps to confirm the argument that there is a significant positive correlation between labour productivity and income per head.

4. A multiple regression analysis

We have seen than one-half of the variation in labour productivity can be explained by reference to variations in the degree of tightness in the la-

bour market. We now examine the extent to which the degrees of expla
tion is improved by postulating that labour productivity is a function of
the four explanatory variables which so far have been discussed separ
ately—the state of the labour market, sales size of shop, market share
multiples and co-operatives, and income per head. The results of the
multiple regression analysis are summarised by giving the equations f
'All Towns' only. These are shown in Table 5.9.

Table 5.9. Results of Multiple Regression Analysis. 160 towns.
1961

| | | Explanatory Variables | | | | |
Equation	Constant	X_1	X_2	X_3	X_4	R^2
1.	3330	120.5 (11.6)	0.041 (0.004)			0.68
2.	2967	146.1 (11.0)		21.75 (2.35)		0.67
3.	2903	124.8 (10.9)	0.027 (0.005)	13.38 (2.67)		0.72
4.	800	63.5 (10.8)	0.026 (0.004)	12.52 (2.12)	4.26 (0.45)	0.82

X_1 = percentage vacancies minus percentage of unemployment
Average 1957-1961.

X_2 = sales per shop.

X_3 = percentage of sales made by multiples and co-operatives

X_4 = income per head.

R^2 = square of the coefficient of multiple correlation, which gives
the overall degree of explanation.(1)

The main results may be summarised as follows. First, the addition of
either sales per shop or the market share of multiples and co-operatives to the labour market variable (Equations 1 and 2) increases the
'explanation' of productivity differences from one-half to two-thirds. In
both equations the regression coefficients of both variables are highly

---

(1) The square of the coefficient of multiple correlation (R^2) is not the
simple addition of the individual r^2s obtained in the simple corre-
lations with only one explanatory variable. This is because of the
duplication that exists between the explanatory variables. For give
values of r^2s the overall degrees of explanation (R^2) will be great
the less duplication there is between the explanatory variables.

70

significant.(1) Because of inter-correlation between the explanatory variables, however, the value of the labour market coefficient is reduced as compared to its value in the simple regression equation (Table 5. 4). Equation 1 tells us that a difference between towns of one per cent in the excess of percentage vacancies over the percentage of unemployment (i.e. +1. 6 per cent instead of +0. 6 per cent) will, size of shop remaining constant, tend to be associated with a difference of £121 in sales per person engaged, and a difference of £100 in sales per shop will, labour market conditions remaining constant, tend to be associated with a difference of £41 in sales per person engaged.

Secondly, looking at equation 3, the inclusion of both size of shop and the market share of multiples and co-operatives is seen to result in a significant increase in the overall degree of explanation, R^2 now being 0. 72. The partial regression coefficients are all highly significant particularly that of the labour market variable. The values of the coefficients for X_2 and X_3 are much reduced as a result of the strong inter-correlation between these two variables. However the fact that both are highly significant suggests that we were justified in including both size of shop and the market share of multiples and co-operatives as explanatory variables in the regression equation.

Thirdly, when income per head is added to the analysis (equation 4) the regression coefficients are again all highly significant and the overall explanation of productivity differences is increased from 72 per cent to 82 per cent. The evidence suggests, therefore, that all four variables contribute significantly to the explanation of differences in labour productivity. As compared to equation 3, however, the value of the regression coefficient for the labour market variable is very markedly reduced

---

(1)   A statistical point which needs to be mentioned here is that the high significance of the regression coefficient for sales per shop may be due to an upward bias as a result of correlating ratios which have a common numerator. In other words a correlation between x/y and x/z of about 0. 5 will be obtained even if x, y and z are independently distributed because x appears in the numerator of both ratios. However in terms of the present analysis which correlates sales per person with sales per shop, while independently distributed values of the two ratios would tend to result in some correlation this is not spurious because sales, persons engaged and number of shops, are not variables which we would expect to be independent of each other. As a check, however, the regression of sales per person engaged on the labour market and size of shop variables has been calculated with size of shop measured in terms of the number of people engaged. The regression equation is $Y = 3645 + 156. 8_{X_1} + 86. 3_{X_2}$ and
$$(12. 7) \qquad (18. 5)$$
the squares of the coefficient of multiple correlation is 0. 58. The regression coefficient for the size of shop variable is still highly significant although less significant than before. Since sales is a better indicator of size of shop than persons engaged we continue, however, to use sales size of shop in the analysis.

Diagram 5. Factors affecting labour productivity: 160 towns, 1961

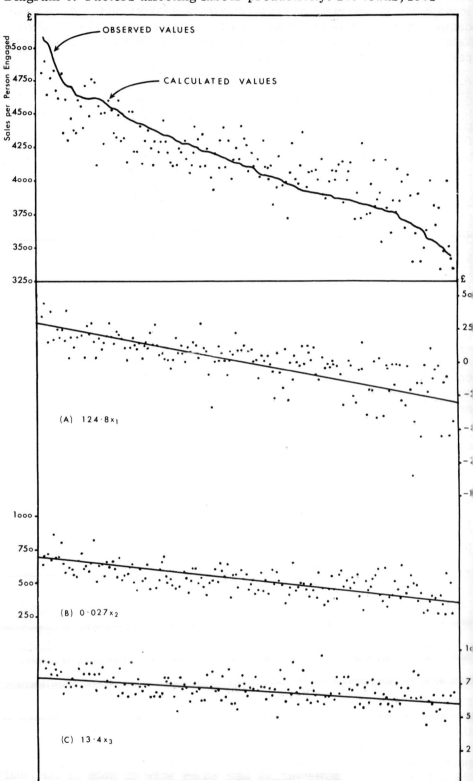

as a result of the high inter-correlation between the labour market and income per head variables. Owing to the unsatisfactory nature of the data on income per head, however, we should not make too much of the values of the regression coefficients for the labour market and income per head variables in equation 4.

A further analysis of the income per head variable is obtained by looking at the 55 towns in size classes (4) and (5) for which figures of the ratio of car licences to households are available, this ratio being used as a proxy measure of income per head. The multiple regression equation for these towns is:

$$Y = 3083 + 122.3_{X_1} + 0.016_{X_2} + 12.50_{X_3} + 1.07_{X_4} \quad R^2 = 0.65$$
$$(21.5) \quad\quad (0.009) \quad (4.49) \quad (4.5)$$

Where X_4 is the ratio of car licences to households. The regression coefficient for the labour market variable is now affected very little by the X_4 variable, and in this equation only the X_1 and X_3 variables have regression coefficients which are highly significant. The significance of the size of shop variable (X_2) is much reduced because of the intercorrelation between it and the ratio of car licences to households (the square of the coefficient of correlation between the two variables being 0.33) and the X_4 variable itself is clearly not significant. This certainly does not prove that income per head is not an important factor in explaining labour productivity. The ratio of car licences to households is, of course, a very indirect measure of income per head, but apart from this the income per head variable may well work indirectly via the size of shop and the market share of multiples, with multiples for instance tending to set up branches more in prosperous towns than in poor ones.

The evidence suggests, then, that all four explanatory factors contribute significantly to the explanation of inter-town productivity differences. It

---

Diagram 5. Factors affecting labour productivity: 160 towns, 1961.

Note: Series A: contribution of the labour market variable to calculated values of sales per person engaged; Series B: contribution of size of shop variable to calculated values of sales per person engaged; Series C: contribution of market share of multiples and co-operatives variable to calculated values of sales per person engaged.

The towns are arranged in descending order of standardised sales per person engaged. For definition of variables see notes to table 5.9, page 70.

The discrepancies between the observed and calculated values of sales per person engaged are nearly all negative for high productivity towns and positive for low productivity ones. This might be due to the omission of the income per head variable, which, if it had been included, might have raised the calculated values of high productivity towns relatively to low productivity ones. Or it might be due to the fact that the influence of, say, the degree of labour shortage on labour productivity is not a linear one.

remains to examine which of the explanatory variables contributes most to the explanation. This depends on how big the inter-town variations are for each variable, and how sensitive productivity is to these variations, other things remaining constant.

The general picture for the three explanatory variables included in equation 3 (Table 5.9.) is shown in Diagram 5.(1) The top part of the diagram shows the observed values of standardised sales per person engaged, and the values which have been calculated from the multiple regression equation. The towns are arranged in descending order of the observed value of standardised sales per person engaged. The lower part of the diagram shows, on the same scale, the contribution of each of the three explanatory variables to the overall explanation.(2) The sum of the three individual components is the calculated series shown in the upper part of the diagram.

It is clear that, of the three explanatory variables, the labour market variable is the one which contributes most to the overall explanation of inter-town productivity differences. As between high and low productivity towns (i.e. the points on the left hand and right hand side of the diagram respectively) there is a wider variation in the values showing the contribution of the labour market variable to the overall explanation of sales per person engaged than there is in the values showing the contribution of the other two variables. This is clearly seen by comparing the slopes of the lines of approximate best fit. For the labour market variable the approximate range of variation is £600 (from £300 to −£300), for the size of shop variable it is £250 (from £600 to £350) and for the market share of multiples and co-operatives variable it is £200 (from £800 to £600).

Although, then, all the variables included in the regression analysis contribute significantly to the overall degree of explanation of inter-town differences in productivity, the evidence suggests that the factor which contributes most to this explanation is inter-town differences in the state of the labour market.

To summarise for all towns, over 80 per cent of the variations in productivity can be 'explained' by postulating that labour productivity is a function of the state of the labour market, size of shop, the market share of multiples and co-operatives, and income per head. The evidence suggests that all four variables contribute significantly to the explanation. Owing to the unsatisfactory nature of the income per head data however and the fact that it shows a substantial degree of correlation with the labour market variable the interpretation of equation 4 (Table 5.9) is subject to some amount of ambiguity. Excluding the income per head variable, we can say that over 70 per cent of the variation in productivity

---

(1) The income per head variable is excluded from this discussion because of the unsatisfactory nature of the data.

(2) The contribution of the labour market variable X_1, for instance, is obtained by multiplying the value of this variable for each town by the value of the partial regression coefficient: 124.8.

has been 'explained', that the labour market variable is highly significant and that although there is a great deal of duplication between the variables, both size of shop and the market share of multiples and co-operatives contribute significantly to the overall explanation.

Kinds of Business

We now turn to see the extent to which the same kind of analysis can 'explain' variations in labour productivity in individual kinds of business. We look first at the simple regression of sales per person engaged on the degree of tightness in the labour market. The size of shop and income per head variables are then taken into account to see the extent to which they improve the overall degree of explanation.(1)

1. The labour market

The regression of sales per person engaged on the excess of percentage vacancies over the percentage of unemployment for each kind of business is shown in Table 5.10. The results can be summarised as follows. First, there are big differences between kinds of business in the value of

Table 5.10. Regression of Sales per Person Engaged on Excess of Percentage Vacancies Over the Percentage of Unemployment. By Kind of Business. 160 Towns 1961

Kind of Business	Constant	Regression Coefficient	r^2
Groceries & Provisions	5254	246.5 (27.0)	0.35
Other Food	4164	262.1 (22.4)	0.46
Confectioners, Tobacc. Newsagents	4361	209.7 (32.4)	0.21
Clothing & Footwear	4093	138.6 (24.3)	0.18
Household Goods	4008	138.5 (22.9)	0.19
Other Non Food	3319	105.0 (13.9)	0.27
General Stores	3363	34.7 (20.1)	0.02

(1) The market share of multiples and co-operatives is not included because the 1961 Census does not distinguish on a town basis between forms of organisation within kinds of business.

the regression coefficients. Thus for Groceries and Provision Dealers
for instance a one per cent increase in the excess of percentage vacancies over the percentage of unemployment tends to be associated with a
increase in sales per person engaged of £247. For Clothing and Footwear on the other hand the same degree of change in labour market con
ditions will tend to lead to an increase of only £139 in sales per person
engaged. Secondly, although the regression coefficients are highly sign
ficant in all kinds of business (apart from General Stores) the degree o
significance is considerably higher for the food trades—Groceries and
Provisions and Other Food—than for the others, and this is reflected in
differences in the size of the squares of the coefficients of correlation.
For the food trades between one-third and one-half of the variations in
sales per person engaged is 'explained' by variations in labour market
conditions, and for the other kinds of business excluding General Stores
only about one-fifth of the variations in sales per person engaged are
'explained' in the same way. The state of the labour market therefore
apparently more important in explaining productivity differences in the
food trades than in other kinds of business.

Thirdly, the degree of 'explanation' is in general, however, much less
than it was for all retail trade, which suggests that in towns where
labour is scarce there is a general raising of efficiency in the use of
labour in the town as a whole (although not equally as between kinds of
business), but as between towns, the effect on individual kinds of busine
is less systematic.

2.   The labour market and sales per shop.

The extent to which the addition of sales size of shop as an explanatory
variable increases the amount of 'explained' variation in labour produc
tivity is shown in Table 5.11. The overall degree of explanation is greatly
increased in the first four kinds of business where the sales per shop
variable is most significant. In Groceries and Provisions for instance
the degree of explanation has increased from 35 per cent to 71 per cen
and the regression equation, $Y = 4004 + 117.3X_1 + 0.06X_2$, tells us tha
a one per cent increase in the excess of percentage vacancies over the
percentage of unemployment will, sales per shop being constant, tend to
be associated with an increase of £117 in sales per person engaged, an
an increase of £1000 in sales per shop, labour market conditions constant, will tend to be associated with an increase of £60 in sales per pe
son engaged. Both regression coefficients are highly significant, but th
value and the significance of the labour market variable are much less
than they were in the simple regression because of the inter-correlatic
between the two explanatory variables.

The same general conclusions apply to the next two kinds of business—
Other Food, and Confectioners, Tobacconists, Newsagents. The overall
degree of explanation is markedly improved by the introduction of the
size of shop variable, and the intercorrelation reduces the values and t
significance of the labour market variable. In the case of Confectioner
etc., the labour market variable no longer appears to be significant and
the entire 'explanation' of productivity differences seems to be attributable to differences in sales per shop. The regression coefficient for t
sales per shop variable is very high compared to what it is for other

Table 5.11. Regression of Sales per Person Engaged on the State of the Labour Market and Size of Shop. By Kind of Business. 160 Towns 1961

| Kind of Business | Constant | Explanatory Variables | | |
		X_1	X_2	R^2
1. Groceries & Provisions	4004	117.3 (20.1)	0.060 (0.004)	0.71
2. Other Food	2980	152.0 (19.9)	0.071 (0.007)	0.70
3. Confectioners etc.	2097	32.7 (25.5)	0.180 (0.013)	0.64
4. Clothing & Footwear	3301	123.7 (19.5)	0.042 (0.004)	0.47
5. Household Goods	3604	134.0 (22.3)	0.023 (0.007)	0.24
6. Other Non Food	3224	102.4 (13.8)	0.007 (0.003)	0.29
7. General	3202	38.6 (19.9)	0.0006 (0.0002)	0.05

X_1 = Percentage Vacancies minus Percentage Unemployed,

X_2 = Sales per Shop.

kinds of business, with an increase of £1000 in sales per shop being associated on average with an increase of £180 in sales per person engaged. There does not appear to be any plausible economic explanation to this statistical result and we should not conclude that the state of the labour market has no effect on labour productivity in this kind of business. The simple regression of sales per person engaged on the labour market variable showed that the regression coefficient is highly significant and there does not seem to be any plausible economic reason why this conclusion should be reversed by bringing size of shop into consideration.

For Clothing and Footwear the introduction of sales per shop again increases substantially the overall degree of explanation—from 18 per cent to 47 per cent. The regression coefficient for the labour market variable is however, not much affected. The equation tells us that a one per cent increase in the excess of percentage vacancies over the percentage of unemployment will, sales per shop constant, tend to be associated with an increase of £124 in sales per person engaged, and an increase of £1000 in sales per shop will, the state of the labour market constant, tend to be associated with an increase of £42 in sales per person engaged.

8. The Labour Market, Sales per Shop and Income per Head

The effect of introducing the income per head variable is shown in Table 5.12. For the food trades three-quarters of the variation in sales per person engaged is now 'explained' by the multiple regression analysis. All three regression coefficients are significant, but the significance of the labour market variable is reduced because of the intercorrelation between it and the income per head variable. Two-thirds of the variation sales per person engaged is explained, for Confectioners etc., and one-half for Clothing and Footwear. In the former the statistical explanation is almost entirely due to the size of shop variable; in the latter, all three regression coefficients are significant. For Household Goods and Other

Table 5.12. Regression of Sales per Person Engaged on the State the Labour Market, Sales per Shop, and Income per Head: by Kind of Business. 160 Towns 1961

| Kind of Business | Constant | Explanatory Variables | | | |
		X_1	X_2	X_3	R^2
1. Groceries & Provisions	375	52.5 (21.9)	0.054 (0.004)	5.21 (0.96)	0.76
2. Other food	−1195	77.2 (20.4)	0.062 (0.006)	6.02 (0.86)	0.77
3. Confectioners etc.	−988	−21.6 (28.7)	0.167 (0.013)	4.51 (1.23)	0.67
4. Clothing & Footwear	952	75.3 (25.1)	0.044 (0.004)	3.21 (1.08)	0.52
5. Household Goods	−853	42.9 (27.3)	0.029 (0.007)	6.05 (1.18)	0.35
6. Other Non Food	1023	56.9 (17.2)	0.008 (0.003)	3.04 (0.74)	0.36
7. General Stores	2851	31.5 (25.9)	0.0006 (0.0002)	0.48 (1.12)	0.05

Non Food the degree of explanation is one-third while for General Stor it is still virtually nil.

To summarise, the overall degree of explanation obtained for Groceries and Provisions, and Other Food is very similar to that obtained for all tail trade. It might well have been better if the market share of multip and co-operatives had been included as an explanatory factor. The deg of explanation is still reasonably good for Confectioners etc., and Cloth ing and Footwear, especially in view of the fact that one important expl atory variable is not included. This might be of particular importance Clothing and Footwear, where in 1961 over 50 per cent of the sales ma by organisations other than co-operative societies were made by multiple which compares, for instance, with about 40 per cent for Groceries and Provisions and 14 per cent for Confectioners etc. For the remaining kinds of business the degree of 'explanation is much less, being about third for Household Goods and Other Non Food and nil for General Stor

5 Some Concluding Comments

3y way of conclusion we give some tentative answers to the questions
which were asked in the introductory chapter.

. For all retail trade, there is no tendency for labour productivity to
e higher for large towns than for small ones; if towns are divided into
road size-classes, a high degree of uniformity is found in average sales
er person engaged.

. If the towns in each size-class are divided into five groups accord-
ıg to their level of labour productivity, we find that the highest produc-
tvity group shows much the same figure for sales per person engaged in
ach size-class, and similarly for the other productivity groups.

. There are big differences in productivity between the towns within
ach size-class and, as indicated above, the dispersion in each class is
nuch the same.

. If separate figures are prepared for each form of organisation—'mul-
iples and co-operatives' and 'independents'—we again find, in each case,
nuch the same average level of labour productivity for each size-class
f town, but big variations between towns within each size-class.

. There is some positive association between the over-all level of
abour productivity in a town and the percentage of its market supplied
y multiples and co-operatives; but the main explanation of inter-town
ifferences in over-all labour productivity is the variation in labour pro-
uctivity within each type of organisation rather than the different pro-
ortions of multiples and co-operatives in high and low productivity
owns.

. In relating labour productivity by kind of business to size of town
he most striking results are the tendency for sales per person engaged
o be negatively correlated with size of town for Groceries and Provi-
ions, and positively correlated with size of town for Clothing and Foot-
vear. These patterns are related to differences between town size-
lasses in the market share of multiples and co-operatives, this share,
n average, decreasing with size of town for Groceries and Provisions,
nd increasing with size of town for Clothing and Footwear.

. The productivity ranking of towns by form of organisation are simi-
ar to the 'overall' ranking. By kind of business, however, the ranking of
owns shows varying degrees of conformity to the overall ranking, being
ood, for instance, for Groceries and Provisions, and Other Food, and
ad for General Stores.

8.   As we would expect, labour productivity is higher in the Central Shopping Areas (C.S.A's) than in the rest of towns, and this on average applies to all kinds of business.

9.   There are marked differences between kinds of business, however, in the relation between labour productivity in C.S.A's and elsewhere. I the grocery trades and in clothing and footwear, the differences in labo productivity between the C.S.A's and elsewhere are greater in high pro ductivity towns than in low productivity ones. For the confectioners, tobacconists, newsagents group on the other hand, the differences are greater in the low productivity towns.

10.   For Groceries and Provisions, and Clothing and Footwear the superiority of high productivity towns is greatest in the central shoppi areas. For the confectioners, tobacconists, newsagents group, however, the superiority of high productivity towns is greatest outside the centr areas.

11.   There are also marked differences between kinds of business in th percentage of sales made in the central shopping areas of towns. For Groceries and Provisions, for instance, the percentage of sales made i the C.S.A's is higher in small towns than in larger ones, and higher in high productivity towns than in low productivity ones. For Clothing and Footwear, on the other hand, the percentage of sales made in C.S.A's shows no marked tendency to vary either with size of town or with the productivity ranking of towns.

12.   There is considerable variability in the relation between the sales size of towns and their population sizes, and considerable variation, therefore, in the sales-inhabitant ratio. The variability within size-classes was explained by reference to variations in income per head a to the varying importance of migrant custom. The relationship betwee sales per inhabitant and size of town varies from one kind of business to another. For Groceries and Provisions, virtually no correlation was found between the two variables. For Clothing and Footwear there was marked positive correlation for towns with sales of Clothing and Foot-wear up to about £4 million.

13.   A high percentage of the workforce (over 30 per cent) in retail tra is employed on a part-time basis. The percentage of the workforce em ployed part-time is greater in large shops than in small ones, and greater i multiples than in other forms of organisation. The greater importance of part-time working in the large establishments of multiples is appar tly due entirely to the greater importance in this type of shop of 'Satur day-only' workers employed to cope with the problem of peak demand.

14.   On a town basis there is a positive correlation between labour pro ductivity and the use of part-time labour which is due to the associatio of high productivity towns with tight labour market conditions. Some o the additional use of part-time labour in towns where labour is scarce might be a short-term measure to relieve labour shortage, the longer run solution being to introduce new methods of selling which make a proportionately smaller use of part-time labour.

15.   The greater part of the employment of part-time labour, however, occurs independently of the state of the labour market. This is becaus

the existence of peaks in demand make it more profitable for shops in <u>all</u> towns to employ part-time rather than full-time labour.

16. The simple regression analysis of labour productivity on the degree of tightness in the labour market suggests that labour market conditions are an important factor in determining efficiency in the use of labour. It is possible of course that labour saving techniques such as self-service would have been introduced in any case, but the findings are consistent with the hypothesis that varying degrees of tightness in the labour market is an important explanatory factor in analysing productivity differences.

17. Bearing in mind the fact that the measure of output used is the value of goods sold it is necessary to point out that the higher sales per person engaged in towns where labour is scarce is likely to be accompanied by a somewhat lower standard of service.

18. The multiple regression analysis which postulates that labour productivity is a function of labour market conditions, size of shop, the market share of multiples and co-operatives, and income per head, suggests that all four explanatory variables are significant in 'explaining' overall productivity differences, the overall degree of explanation being over 80 per cent.

19. The labour market variable is the one which contributes most to the overall explanation of inter-town differences in productivity.

20. The unsatisfactory nature of the data on income per head, however, make it difficult to analyse the importance of this factor as a determinant of labour productivity. But it is certainly very plausible to argue that along with the state of the labour market it is a more fundamental factor than sales per shop and the market share of multiples, in explaining differences in labour productivity.

21. The use of the multiple regression analysis to explain productivity differences between towns in individual kinds of business meets with varying degrees of success. The overall degree of explanation is for instance, about 75 per cent for the food trades, 50 per cent for Clothing and Footwear and only 35 per cent for Household Goods. These figures compare to an overall degree of explanation of 82 per cent for all retail trade. The lower degree of explanation by kinds of business is in part due to the fact that in the kind of business analysis there is one less explanatory factor, the market share of multiples and co-operatives being omitted because of lack of data. If we look at the degrees of explanation with two explanatory variables (the labour market and size of shop) then the degree of explanation for all retail trade (68 per cent) is exceeded by that for two kinds of business—Groceries and Provisions, and Other Food (the degree of explanation being 71 per cent and 70 per cent respectively).

21. It is worth noting that of the explanatory variables, two—the size of shop and the market share of multiples and co-operatives—are subject to management control, and two—the state of the labour market and income per head—are largely environmental in the sense of being outside the control of management. It would seem that an increase in the importance of multiple stores would have a beneficial effect on labour pro-

ductivity. However, although these stores can be expected to grow in in portance it must also be remembered that there are limits to the exten to which it is feasible to extend their operation. The success of this type of shop depends on high turnover and there are a number of factor such as low income sections of the community, fragmentation of the ma ket caused by product differentiation associated with high incomes, and low density population areas, which militate against the establishment c environments suitable for chain store operation.

As to the environmental variables it might be expected that a successfu policy of regional development would improve the productivity perform ance in low productivity towns by increasing the degree of labour scar- city, and also income per head.

23. There is one aspect of the labour market, however, which is not out side the scope of management control, and that is the extent to which it is prepared to take action to increase the quality of labour. This can be accomplished by encouraging staff to attend educational courses, and by making conditions of work, especially with regard to working hours and fringe benefits, more comparable with those in industry and commerce

Appendix A
Towns Included in the Analysis

Town	Size-Class	Reference Number*	Town	Size-Class	Reference Number*
Aberdeen	5	32	Chester	4	28
Ayr	1	25	Chesterfield	3	28
Barking	1	3	Chislehurst	1	12
Barnsley	3	22	Colchester	2	17
Barrow	1	30	Coventry	5	4
Basildon	1	17	Crewe	1	23
Bath	4	27	Dagenham	2	3
Bedford	3	7	Darlington	3	27
Bexley	3	6	Derby	5	10
Birkenhead	4	30	Doncaster	4	17
Birmingham	5	7	Dudley	2	8
Blackburn	4	34	Dundee	5	34
Blackpool	5	21	Ealing	5	1
Bolton	4	31	Eastbourne	3	16
Bournemouth	5	29	East Ham	4	9
Bradford	5	30	Edinburgh	5	23
Brighton	5	8	Edmonton	2	4
Bristol	5	20	Enfield	3	3
Bromley	4	7	Exeter	4	26
Burnley	2	30	Finchley	2	2
Burton on Trent	1	21	Gateshead	2	26
Cambridge	4	11	Glasgow	5	26
Canterbury	1	10	Gloucester	3	18
Cardiff	5	16	Gravesend	2	12
Carlisle	3	23	Greenock	1	29
Chatham	2	6	Grimsby	4	29
Cheltenham	3	13	Guildford	3	2
Chelmsford	2	9	Halifax	3	25

Equal to rank order within the size-class for standardised sales per person engaged

83

Town	Size-Class	Reference Number*	Town	Size-Class	Reference Number*
Harrogate	2	22	Norwich	5	22
Harrow	5	5	Nottingham	5	15
Hastings	2	27	Nuneaton	1	11
Hereford	1	15	Oldham	4	32
Hendon	4	10	Orpington	1	8
Heston	3	4	Oxford	4	6
High Wycombe	1	2	Paisley	3	24
Hornchurch	2	7	Perth	1	31
Hornsey	1	9	Peterborough	3	17
Hove	2	18	Plymouth	5	28
Huddersfield	4	21	Poole	2	19
Ilford	5	6	Portsmouth	5	18
Ipswich	4	20	Preston	4	24
Kingston upon Hull	5	27	Reading	5	2
			Rhondda	2	31
Kilmarnock	1	28	Richmond	1	6
Kirkaldy	1	24	Rochdale	2	23
Leeds	5	9	Romford	4	2
Leicester	5	13	Rotherham	3	21
Leyton	3	8	Royal Leamington Spa	1	16
Lincoln	3	11			
Liverpool	5	24			
Luton	4	5	Royal Tunbridge Wells	2	16
Maidstone	2	13	Ruislip	1	7
Manchester	5	14	St. Albans	2	1
Mansfield	2	15	St. Helens	3	20
Middlesbrough	4	22	Salford	4	33
Motherwell	2	14	Salisbury	1	18
Newcastle under Lyme	1	26	Scarborough	2	29
			Scunthorpe	1	20
Newcastle upon Tyne	5	12	Sheffield	5	25
Newport (Mon.)	4	13	Shrewsbury	1	22
Northampton	4	18	Slough	4	3

84

Town	Size-Class	Reference Number*	Town	Size-Class	Reference Number*
Smethwick	1	19	Uxbridge	1	4
Solihull	1	13	Wakefield	2	20
Southampton	5	19	Wallasey	2	28
Southend	5	11	Walsall	4	14
Southgate	2	10	Walthamstow	3	15
Southport	3	30	Warrington	3	19
South Shields	3	29	Watford	4	4
Staines	1	1	Wembley	4	1
Stockport	4	23	West Bromwich	3	5
Stockton	3	14	West Ham	4	15
Stoke on Trent	5	31	West Hartlepool	2	24
Sunderland	5	33	Wigan	3	26
Surbiton	1	5	Willesden	4	12
Sutton & Cheam	4	8	Wimbledon	2	11
Swansea	5	17	Woking	1	14
Swindon	4	16	Wolverhampton	5	3
Thurrock	2	5	Wood Green	3	1
Torquay	2	25	Worcester	3	12
Tottenham	3	10	Worthing	4	19
Twickenham	3	9	Yarmouth	2	21
Tynemouth	1	27	York	4	25

Appendix B
Population, Turnover, and Sales per Person Engaged: All Retail Trade

1. <u>Towns with Turnover of £10m. and under £12.25m.</u>

Town	Overall Productivity Ranking (a)	(b)	Population '000	Turnover Total £'000	Per Inhabitant	Sales per Person Engaged (Full-time Equivalent) £'000 All Shops (a)	(b)	Independents	Mu &Co-
Staines	1	4	49.3	10.7	217	4.81	4.83	3.95	5.6
High Wycombe	2	7	50.3	12.1	240	4.72	4.69	3.95	5.7
Barking	3	2	72.3	10.7	148	4.70	4.90	4.32	5.4
Uxbridge	4	6	63.8	10.1	158	4.70	4.73	4.25	5.2
Surbiton	5	1	62.9	10.4	165	4.61	5.00	4.08	5.9
Richmond	6	8	41.0	10.4	253	4.61	4.59	3.84	5.0
Ruislip	7	3	72.5	11.2	155	4.59	4.87	4.08	5.5
Orpington	8	5	80.3	11.3	141	4.53	4.76	4.12	5.4
Hornsey	9	9	97.9	10.8	111	4.37	4.56	3.29	5.5
Canterbury	10	16	30.4	11.0	361	4.35	4.14	3.62	4.8
Nuneaton	11	14	56.6	11.4	202	4.31	4.24	3.88	4.6
Chislehurst	12	10	86.9	10.8	125	4.27	4.54	4.13	5.0
Solihull	13	11	96.0	10.5	110	4.22	4.46	3.95	5.2
Woking	14	12	67.5	11.4	168	4.22	4.35	3.87	5.0
Hereford	15	17	40.4	10.2	252	4.13	4.08	3.78	4.5
Royal L. Spa	16	18	43.2	11.4	263	4.13	4.03	3.80	4.4
Basildon	17	13	88.5	11.4	129	4.05	4.26	3.90	4.
Salisbury	18	23	35.5	11.1	312	4.03	3.88	3.41	4.
Smethwick	19	15	68.4	12.1	177	3.99	4.15	3.78	4.6
Scunthorpe	20	20	67.3	12.0	178	3.92	3.96	3.34	4.
Burton on Trent	21	19	50.8	11.2	221	3.91	3.99	3.60	4.
Shrewsbury	22	22	49.7	11.7	234	3.91	3.90	3.44	4.
Crewe	23	21	53.4	10.5	197	3.86	3.90	3.36	4.
Kirkaldy	24	24	52.4	10.7	204	3.86	3.86	3.35	4.
Ayr	25	27	45.3	12.1	268	3.77	3.73	3.55	3.
Newcastle U. Lyme	26	25	76.4	11.0	144	3.76	3.85	3.46	4.
Tynemouth	27	26	70.1	10.1	145	3.69	3.79	3.41	4.
Kilmarnock	28	28	47.5	10.0	211	3.66	3.72	3.34	4.
Greenock	29	29	74.6	10.8	145	3.66	3.71	3.43	3.
Barrow	30	30	64.8	10.2	158	3.56	3.60	3.13	4.
Perth	31	31	41.2	11.1	270	3.47	3.36	3.00	3.
Average			61.2	11.0	196	4.14	4.21	3.69	4.

(a) Standardised sales per person engaged.   (b) 'Crude' sales per person engaged

Appendix B—(continued)

2. Towns with Turnover of £12.25m. and under £15m.

Town	Overall Productivity Ranking (a)	(b)	Population '000	Turnover Total £'000	Per Inhabitant	Sales per Person Engaged (Full-time Equivalent) £'000 All Shops (a)	(b)	Independents	Mult. & Co-ops
St. Albans	1	2	50.3	13.2	262	4.93	4.86	3.99	5.70
Finchley	2	3	69.3	13.7	198	4.70	4.77	4.14	5.49
Dagenham	3	1	108.4	13.2	121	4.63	4.92	4.46	5.28
Edmonton	4	5	92.1	13.5	147	4.48	4.68	4.24	5.24
Thurrock	5	6	114.3	14.8	138	4.46	4.55	4.22	4.83
Chatham	6	8	49.0	12.3	251	4.44	4.44	3.46	5.12
Hornchurch	7	4	128.1	14.3	111	4.43	4.73	4.31	5.25
Dudley	8	9	61.7	13.3	215	4.43	4.43	3.80	5.03
Chelmsford	9	10	49.8	12.5	250	4.42	4.40	3.54	5.58
Southgate	10	7	72.1	13.0	181	4.39	4.52	4.01	5.07
Wimbledon	11	14	57.0	12.3	215	4.35	4.25	3.60	5.20
Gravesend	12	11	51.4	12.4	242	4.33	4.31	3.75	4.84
Maidstone	13	15	59.8	14.7	247	4.27	4.20	3.85	4.55
Motherwell	14	12	72.8	13.1	179	4.22	4.29	3.35	5.06
Mansfield	15	13	53.2	14.1	265	4.22	4.27	3.56	4.85
R. Tunbridge Wells	16	19	39.9	12.9	324	4.18	4.00	3.30	5.06
Colchester	17	16	65.1	14.7	226	4.17	4.19	3.36	5.02
Hove	18	17	72.8	13.8	190	3.97	4.09	3.63	4.69
Poole	19	18	88.1	13.3	151	3.94	4.05	3.89	4.27
Wakefield	20	20	61.6	14.5	235	3.91	3.93	3.54	4.39
Gt. Yarmouth	21	22	52.9	13.2	249	3.89	3.84	3.36	4.46
Harrogate	22	25	56.3	14.5	257	3.83	3.75	3.32	4.55
Rochdale	23	23	85.8	13.9	162	3.82	3.82	3.37	4.71
W. Hartlepool	24	24	77.1	13.2	172	3.82	3.78	3.38	4.15
Torquay	25	26	53.9	13.0	242	3.82	3.72	3.26	4.24
Gateshead	26	21	103.2	14.5	140	3.64	3.90	3.34	4.38
Hastings	27	29	66.3	13.2	199	3.55	3.55	3.06	4.28
Wallasey	28	27	103.2	12.0	126	3.52	3.69	3.07	4.69
Scarborough	29	31	42.6	12.6	297	3.52	3.45	2.97	4.34
Burnley	30	30	80.6	13.9	172	3.51	3.51	3.25	4.12
Rhondda	31	28	100.3	12.2	122	3.33	3.56	3.05	4.29
Average			72.2	13.4	203	4.10	4.14	3.59	4.80

3. <u>Towns with Turnover of £15m. and under £19m.</u>

Town	Overall Productivity Ranking (a)	(b)	Population '000	Turnover Total £'000	Per Inhabitant	Sales per Person Engaged (Full-time Equivalent) £'000 All Shops (a)	(b)	Independents	Mul & Co-
Wood Green	1	1	47.9	14.9	311	5.08	5.17	4.10	5.8
Guildford	2	7	54.0	17.3	321	4.74	4.58	3.79	5.2
Enfield	3	4	109.5	17.8	162	4.63	4.73	4.10	5.4
Heston	4	5	102.9	18.5	180	4.63	4.65	3.95	5.1
West Bromwich	5	3	95.9	15.4	160	4.61	4.77	4.36	5.2
Bexley	6	6	89.6	15.7	176	4.59	4.65	3.83	5.2
Bedford	7	8	63.3	16.6	262	4.43	4.48	3.83	5.2
Leyton	8	10	93.9	16.4	175	4.37	4.43	3.81	5.3
Twickenham	9	2	100.8	16.1	160	4.35	4.85	3.93	6.2
Tottenham	10	9	113.1	18.0	159	4.29	4.46	4.12	5.0
Lincoln	11	13	77.1	18.1	235	4.26	4.16	3.46	5.2
Worcester	12	12	65.9	16.2	245	4.24	4.25	3.72	4.7
Cheltenham	13	18	72.0	18.6	259	4.24	4.06	3.54	4.7
Stockton	14	17	81.2	16.6	204	4.22	4.09	3.58	4.6
Walthamstow	15	11	108.7	17.8	163	4.13	4.31	3.88	5.6
Eastbourne	16	19	60.9	16.7	274	4.12	4.02	3.43	4.5
Peterborough	17	15	62.0	15.0	241	4.09	4.10	3.64	4.6
Gloucester	18	22	69.7	18.1	260	4.07	3.93	3.38	4.5
Warrington	19	14	75.5	16.8	222	4.03	4.14	3.42	5.0
St. Helens	20	16	108.3	17.3	160	3.98	4.10	3.41	5.0
Rotherham	21	21	85.3	16.1	189	3.95	3.95	3.44	4.6
Barnsley	22	20	74.7	18.9	254	3.89	4.01	2.87	4.8
Carlisle	23	24	71.1	17.4	245	3.86	3.86	3.55	4.2
Paisley	24	25	95.8	16.9	177	3.80	3.86	3.43	4.2
Halifax	25	23	96.1	17.1	178	3.79	3.90	3.39	4.
Wigan	26	26	78.7	18.7	237	3.77	3.87	3.48	4.3
Darlington	27	28	84.2	18.2	216	3.75	3.74	3.42	4.6
Chesterfield	28	27	67.8	15.9	234	3.69	3.76	3.14	4.
South Shields	29	29	109.5	16.9	154	3.64	3.70	3.50	3.
Southport	30	30	82.0	17.5	214	3.52	3.55	3.15	4.
Average			83.2	17.1	214	4.16	4.20	3.62	4.

4. Towns with Turnover of £19m. and under £30m.

Town	Overall Productivity Ranking (a)	(b)	Population '000	Turnover Total £'000	Per Inhabitant	Sales per Person Engaged (Full-time Equivalent) £'000 All Shops (a)	(b)	Independents	Mult. & Co-ops
Wembley	1	1	124.8	23.6	189	5.03	5.24	4.55	5.73
Romford	2	2	114.6	25.3	221	5.03	5.07	4.01	5.77
Slough	3	3	80.5	19.4	241	4.88	4.91	4.43	5.19
Watford	4	8	75.6	23.6	312	4.83	4.67	3.91	5.31
Luton	5	6	131.5	25.5	194	4.65	4.69	4.02	5.28
Oxford	6	10	106.1	29.8	280	4.63	4.61	4.06	5.22
Bromley	7	7	68.2	19.3	283	4.61	4.67	3.73	4.40
Sutton & Cheam	8	11	79.0	19.5	246	4.61	4.55	3.98	4.89
East Ham	9	9	105.4	19.5	185	4.57	4.63	4.31	4.95
Hendon	10	5	151.5	27.1	179	4.53	4.78	4.28	5.25
Cambridge	11	12	95.4	25.5	268	4.53	4.41	3.99	4.77
Willesden	12	4	170.8	26.1	153	4.51	4.82	4.62	5.06
Newport	13	13	108.1	22.4	207	4.33	4.37	3.99	4.73
Walsall	14	14	117.8	24.7	210	4.29	4.36	3.85	4.80
West Ham	15	15	157.2	25.2	161	4.26	4.28	4.08	4.54
Swindon	16	18	91.7	23.4	255	4.17	4.07	3.49	5.08
Doncaster	17	16	86.4	25.9	299	4.10	4.13	3.99	4.27
Northampton	18	17	105.4	24.4	231	4.10	4.09	3.69	4.62
Worthing	19	19	80.1	19.8	247	4.10	4.06	3.50	4.86
Ipswich	20	20	117.3	26.0	222	4.03	4.01	3.40	4.97
Huddersfield	21	21	130.3	24.7	190	4.00	4.00	3.51	4.91
Middlesbrough	22	24	157.3	28.8	183	4.00	3.87	3.46	4.24
Stockport	23	22	142.5	23.0	162	3.88	3.92	3.44	4.78
Preston	24	23	113.2	26.3	232	3.88	3.89	3.38	4.66
York	25	25	104.5	24.5	235	3.88	3.87	3.38	4.60
Exeter	26	31	80.2	19.9	248	3.88	3.77	3.43	4.21
Bath	27	29	80.9	19.2	238	3.86	3.81	3.26	4.61
Chester	28	32	59.3	19.8	333	3.85	3.70	3.36	3.99
Grimsby	29	30	96.7	19.6	203	3.82	3.80	3.44	4.42
Birkenhead	30	26	141.7	22.7	160	3.79	3.82	3.27	4.64
Bolton	31	27	160.9	29.6	184	3.77	3.82	3.23	4.93
Oldham	32	33	115.4	19.4	168	3.61	3.65	3.21	4.74
Salford	33	28	155.0	19.1	123	3.57	3.82	3.57	4.48
Blackburn	34	34	106.1	19.0	179	3.53	3.56	3.09	4.63
Average			112.1	23.3	218	4.21	4.23	3.73	4.84

5. Towns with Turnover of £30m. and Over

Town	Overall Productivity Ranking (a)	(b)	Population '000	Turnover Total £'000	Per Inhabitant	Sales per Person Engaged (Full-time Equivalent) £'000 — All Shops (a)	(b)	Independents	Mult & Co-c
Ealing	1	1	183.2	33.6	183	4.55	4.66	3.80	5.62
Reading	2	6	119.9	34.1	284	4.51	4.42	3.91	4.75
Wolverhampton	3	5	150.4	39.6	263	4.46	4.46	3.96	5.19
Coventry	4	4	303.1	53.5	175	4.41	4.47	4.21	4.74
Harrow	5	2	209.0	34.0	163	4.39	4.65	4.15	5.17
Ilford	6	3	178.2	34.9	196	4.33	4.49	3.96	4.94
Birmingham	7	7	1,105.7	203.9	184	4.33	4.37	3.91	4.78
Brighton	8	10	162.8	39.2	241	4.27	4.23	3.54	5.07
Leeds	9	9	510.6	96.2	188	4.22	4.24	3.72	4.87
Derby	10	8	132.3	35.5	268	4.18	4.28	3.58	5.28
Southend	11	12	165.0	34.3	208	4.15	4.18	3.65	4.98
Newcastle	12	13	269.4	78.9	293	4.15	4.05	3.42	4.53
Leicester	13	11	273.3	64.4	236	4.13	4.20	3.68	4.82
Manchester	14	15	661.0	140.1	212	4.05	4.04	3.63	4.53
Nottingham	15	14	311.6	69.6	223	4.03	4.05	3.50	4.70
Cardiff	16	18	256.3	51.5	201	4.03	3.94	3.58	4.45
Swansea	17	16	166.7	30.4	182	4.02	4.02	3.60	4.53
Portsmouth	18	28	215.2	46.5	216	4.00	3.83	3.27	4.25
Southampton	19	19	204.7	45.7	223	3.97	3.91	3.61	4.10
Bristol	20	17	436.4	81.9	188	3.94	3.96	3.66	4.29
Blackpool	21	20	152.1	36.5	240	3.92	3.90	3.53	4.45
Norwich	22	26	119.9	31.3	261	3.89	3.84	3.40	4.53
Edinburgh	23	24	468.4	99.9	213	3.86	3.87	3.40	4.35
Liverpool	24	27	747.5	135.7	182	3.86	3.83	3.56	4.06
Sheffield	25	23	493.9	89.1	180	3.85	3.87	3.44	4.40
Glasgow	26	21	1,054.9	190.0	180	3.83	3.89	3.62	4.14
Hull	27	25	303.3	54.2	179	3.82	3.85	3.52	4.40
Plymouth	28	30	204.3	39.0	191	3.82	3.77	3.24	4.31
Bournemouth	29	32	153.9	42.8	278	3.80	3.72	3.25	4.35
Bradford	30	22	295.8	51.6	175	3.76	3.88	3.46	4.69
Stoke	31	29	265.5	44.0	166	3.70	3.78	3.58	4.07
Aberdeen	32	31	185.4	39.5	213	3.70	3.75	3.26	4.28
Sunderland	33	33	189.6	34.1	180	3.65	3.62	3.42	3.88
Dundee	34	34	183.0	33.1	181	3.45	3.54	3.24	3.91
Average			318.6	63.8	210	4.03	4.05	3.60	4.57

Appendix C

Sales per Person Engaged (Full-time Equivalent) and Percentage of Total Sales: by Kind of Business

1. Towns with Turnover of £10m. and under £12.25m.

Town Ref. No. ‡	Sales per Person Engaged £'000*†							Percentage of Total Sales for Town						
	G.& P.D.	O.F.	C.T. N.	C.& F.	H.G.	O.N. F.	G.S.	G.& P.D.	O.F.	C.T. N.	C.& F.	H.G.	O.N. F.	G.S.
1	6.22	5.38	4.51	4.69	4.59	3.63	3.61	22.7	21.6	9.3	14.7	15.4	6.7	9.6
2	6.01	4.79	4.69	4.88	4.42	3.90	3.50	23.2	20.9	6.4	17.2	12.5	8.6	11.1
3	6.50	4.70	5.18	4.58	4.86	3.54	3.10	25.4	20.9	13.7	14.5	14.4	7.9	3.2
4	6.20	5.32	5.46	3.91	4.30	3.77	3.58	22.8	21.2	13.1	11.4	12.0	7.4	12.1
5	6.75	5.71	5.12	3.50	4.21	3.50	3.33	28.4	29.1	11.4	9.1	10.3	6.5	5.2
6	6.60	5.13	4.52	4.99	4.15	3.72	2.77	20.9	21.9	8.4	19.0	11.0	8.3	10.5
7	6.34	5.34	5.36	4.00	4.22	*	*	25.4	25.0	13.3	12.7	11.7	*	*
8	6.15	4.91	4.63	3.70	4.30	3.87	3.61	28.3	30.6	9.2	10.2	9.3	8.4	4.1
9	6.29	4.54	5.49	3.65	4.25	3.26	3.16	27.2	25.2	11.6	8.8	12.2	8.3	6.6
10	5.55	4.19	4.40	4.62	4.56	3.50	3.01	17.9	12.1	5.4	20.2	16.8	7.9	19.6
11	5.32	4.29	4.35	4.06	4.52	3.74	3.29	24.8	20.2	6.0	16.2	9.9	7.7	15.2
12	6.13	4.88	4.84	3.81	3.92	3.29	2.81	28.2	26.9	11.7	10.5	9.4	7.6	5.7
13	5.30	4.90	4.69	3.49	3.78	*	*	31.4	25.7	8.9	10.7	12.9	*	*
14	5.17	4.48	5.25	3.74	3.69	*	*	25.8	26.7	10.4	13.7	11.7	*	*
15	4.69	3.96	4.92	4.17	4.05	3.32	3.58	22.0	14.0	7.0	19.6	15.2	8.1	14.1
16	5.11	3.59	4.99	4.42	4.08	3.50	3.24	18.4	13.5	6.6	21.2	14.7	7.5	18.0
17	5.77	4.62	4.80	3.43	4.31	3.17	2.48	31.1	20.2	11.9	9.6	15.0	5.1	7.2
18	4.97	4.24	3.87	3.84	3.65	3.21	3.58	15.0	16.8	5.1	19.7	17.7	9.9	15.7
19	4.87	4.30	4.55	3.43	4.50	*	*	24.3	29.7	9.1	13.8	13.4	*	*
20	4.82	4.38	2.75	3.71	4.18	3.56	3.27	26.0	17.7	6.8	18.5	14.2	7.1	9.7
21	5.11	4.14	3.20	3.68	3.97	2.93	3.39	27.2	19.9	5.7	19.2	14.7	6.4	6.9
22	4.63	3.42	4.57	4.40	3.93	3.12	3.16	21.8	14.6	7.6	23.4	10.7	9.5	12.4
23	5.45	3.94	3.12	3.73	3.71	3.00	3.14	27.1	16.3	7.0	17.5	15.1	6.4	10.6
24	5.09	3.64	4.40	4.18	3.39	2.49	3.42	21.2	19.9	8.5	21.0	10.3	6.2	12.9
25	4.70	3.11	4.31	4.03	3.75	2.94	2.91	18.7	14.4	9.2	21.4	16.0	8.6	11.7
26	5.04	3.82	3.64	3.24	3.53	3.17	3.30	33.4	16.7	6.9	15.4	8.2	7.2	12.1
27	4.85	3.77	3.77	2.84	4.16	2.85	3.28	33.0	19.0	9.1	13.1	9.4	4.7	11.7
28	4.92	2.74	3.92	3.71	3.76	3.58	3.39	23.6	12.9	8.5	21.8	11.5	7.4	14.4
29	4.41	3.28	4.37	3.82	3.45	3.06	3.09	27.1	16.3	9.7	20.6	8.0	5.5	12.7
30	4.51	2.97	3.55	3.59	3.74	2.65	3.65	29.8	18.0	7.3	18.9	11.3	7.0	7.7
31	4.73	2.91	3.94	3.49	3.48	3.05	2.71	17.8	18.6	6.9	16.5	15.2	11.2	13.7
Average	5.43	4.25	4.42	3.91	4.05	3.31	3.24	24.8	20.2	8.8	16.1	12.6	7.5	10.9

* Not available

† Full-time equivalent (2 part-time workers = 1 full-time worker)

‡ Descending order of standardised sales per person engaged

G.& P.D. = Grocers and Provision Dealers; O.F. = Other Food; C.T.N. = Confectioners Tobacconists, Newsagents; C.& F. = Clothing and Footwear; H.G. = Household Goods; O.N.F. = Other Non Food; G.S. = General Stores.

2. Towns with Turnover of £12.25m. and under £15m.

Town Ref. No. ‡	G.& P.D.	O.F.	C.T. N.	C.& F.	H.G.	O.N. F.	G.S.	G.& P.D.	O.F.	C.T. N.	C.& F.	H.G.	O.N. F.	G.S.
	Sales per Person Engaged £'000†							Percentage of Total Sales for Town						
1	6.20	5.17	5.64	5.19	4.53	3.23	3.86	21.9	18.3	7.3	20.0	14.5	8.5	9.4
2	6.45	4.82	5.03	4.17	4.29	3.52	3.88	25.0	28.0	9.1	10.9	13.6	8.2	5.2
3	6.23	4.80	6.56	4.07	4.19	3.56	3.26	24.3	31.3	15.0	7.2	12.1	5.5	4.7
4	5.94	4.92	4.89	4.24	4.52	3.42	2.89	23.9	27.4	10.2	14.2	13.7	6.7	3.8
5	5.58	4.28	5.09	4.37	4.34	3.78	3.48	28.4	24.4	12.7	11.0	7.7	5.6	10.2
6	5.80	4.71	3.95	4.39	4.37	3.26	3.57	22.5	20.1	5.7	19.9	13.9	8.4	9.4
7	6.47	4.45	5.12	3.78	4.47	*	*	31.1	23.2	12.3	7.7	13.9	*	*
8	5.10	5.21	3.94	4.19	3.70	3.54	4.30	18.6	23.5	5.1	18.5	11.6	6.2	16.7
9	6.14	4.68	5.05	4.83	4.34	*	*	22.7	17.9	5.8	20.6	16.4	*	*
10	6.33	4.88	5.00	3.56	3.82	3.63	3.10	27.0	22.0	11.5	13.2	11.6	8.7	6.0
11	6.10	4.58	5.35	4.21	3.91	3.06	2.95	20.2	24.6	10.0	11.3	12.8	8.3	12.7
12	5.46	4.12	4.36	4.37	4.32	3.03	3.97	22.7	20.6	6.9	18.3	10.1	6.8	14.6
13	5.42	3.99	4.08	4.36	4.09	3.68	3.59	20.6	17.8	6.5	20.0	11.0	8.4	15.7
14	5.46	3.62	3.95	4.25	4.22	3.59	4.13	29.3	20.9	7.8	15.6	8.8	4.6	13.0
15	5.15	4.42	3.37	4.04	4.47	3.16	3.94	22.3	22.0	4.1	19.1	14.2	5.6	12.8
16	5.27	5.03	4.11	3.68	4.29	3.11	3.01	17.0	18.9	5.5	21.5	14.6	8.7	13.9
17	5.61	3.71	4.34	4.46	3.65	3.67	3.37	23.5	16.4	6.8	22.4	13.1	8.7	9.1
18	5.64	4.43	4.29	3.10	3.63	2.99	3.16	21.2	32.9	11.2	8.7	11.3	7.2	7.5
19	4.85	4.03	4.80	3.48	4.01	3.14	3.03	29.0	22.5	9.7	12.0	13.6	7.1	6.1
20	4.62	3.71	4.27	3.66	4.29	3.12	3.34	24.3	16.7	5.8	18.9	19.0	7.6	7.7
21	5.11	3.41	4.06	4.38	3.42	2.74	3.87	20.9	19.3	7.7	12.5	9.3	9.6	20.7
22	4.48	4.12	4.61	3.62	3.24	3.36	3.11	19.3	20.3	6.5	20.6	13.4	10.0	10.0
23	4.12	3.95	3.74	3.66	3.71	3.18	3.93	29.8	15.2	8.4	16.6	16.2	6.8	7.0
24	5.02	3.74	3.28	4.03	4.01	2.96	2.89	27.8	19.3	6.6	12.5	10.4	5.9	17.4
25	4.89	3.87	4.10	3.72	3.23	3.23	3.07	18.7	20.5	7.9	17.8	11.7	12.2	11.1
26	4.63	3.31	4.07	3.14	3.46	2.70	4.29	33.6	19.5	7.2	5.9	7.8	4.1	22.0
27	5.21	3.29	3.47	3.50	3.07	2.62	3.14	24.4	21.2	9.3	17.7	9.9	8.7	8.8
28	4.99	3.42	3.79	2.96	3.47	2.58	3.06	32.9	23.3	12.8	10.0	9.3	6.7	4.9
29	4.61	3.27	3.88	3.92	3.25	2.91	2.75	18.8	15.9	9.7	17.0	11.4	9.9	17.4
30	3.94	3.61	3.44	3.46	3.24	2.79	3.56	26.6	16.5	9.1	18.5	14.1	6.9	8.3
31	4.36	3.37	2.75	3.12	3.59	2.97	2.60	42.3	18.5	8.8	11.5	9.6	5.3	3.8
Average	5.33	4.16	4.33	3.93	3.91	3.19	3.41	24.9	21.3	8.5	15.2	12.3	7.5	10.7

3. Towns with Turnover of £15m. and under £19m.

Town Ref. No. ‡	Sales per Person Engaged £'000†							Percentage of Total Sales for Town						
	G.& P.D.	O.F.	C.T. N.	C.& F.	H.G.	O.N. F.	G.S.	G.& P.D.	O.F.	C.T. N.	C.& F.	H.G.	O.N. F.	G.S.
1	6.42	4.67	5.10	6.27	4.60	3.44	4.53	13.2	16.4	6.4	31.2	10.0	4.8	17.9
2	5.99	5.34	5.09	5.13	3.85	4.00	3.53	16.3	17.0	5.9	21.2	11.6	9.7	18.3
3	6.33	4.62	5.44	4.14	4.58	3.65	3.79	24.0	26.0	10.6	11.8	9.6	6.9	11.2
4	6.11	4.88	5.45	5.08	4.40	3.53	3.16	21.9	19.3	10.5	17.1	11.2	6.6	13.4
5	5.02	5.31	4.36	4.58	4.61	3.96	3.87	18.6	33.7	6.4	17.1	11.9	6.0	6.3
6	6.24	5.09	4.18	4.13	4.04	3.15	4.53	20.5	24.1	7.6	10.6	12.3	6.0	19.0
7	6.08	4.26	4.56	4.61	4.36	3.49	3.39	22.4	14.3	6.4	21.9	17.3	7.8	9.8
8	5.79	4.64	5.20	3.92	4.18	3.59	3.39	23.9	22.1	10.6	10.7	11.6	6.6	14.4
9	5.18	4.61	5.10	3.56	7.75	3.24	3.11	21.1	25.8	12.2	7.7	21.8	6.8	4.5
10	6.20	4.58	5.23	3.90	4.08	3.34	3.09	22.1	24.7	13.0	12.1	13.3	7.3	7.5
11	4.88	4.73	4.13	4.51	4.35	3.26	3.32	19.8	19.8	6.0	16.3	11.3	8.0	18.7
12	5.55	4.68	3.99	3.84	4.18	3.33	3.57	22.1	19.7	7.1	19.7	12.5	8.6	10.3
13	5.55	4.30	4.51	4.07	4.34	3.43	3.24	19.3	14.6	5.6	19.2	10.5	8.7	22.0
14	4.92	4.39	4.58	4.38	4.64	3.64	3.00	20.2	17.3	6.1	18.4	11.5	7.2	19.3
15	5.38	4.47	5.26	3.81	4.12	3.28	3.02	20.7	24.7	11.7	16.5	14.5	8.0	3.9
16	5.57	4.23	4.42	4.13	4.09	3.27	2.96	19.2	19.5	8.4	18.4	9.5	9.3	15.7
17	4.88	3.95	3.95	4.08	4.06	3.35	3.91	22.4	23.1	5.4	19.5	12.1	8.1	9.4
18	5.18	3.93	4.11	4.47	3.98	3.33	3.14	21.7	13.6	6.5	15.3	10.2	8.9	23.9
19	5.22	3.93	3.68	3.97	3.93	3.39	3.59	29.8	16.2	6.0	18.1	12.4	7.1	10.5
20	5.38	4.49	3.98	4.06	4.07	2.78	3.81	29.7	18.5	6.6	15.2	11.2	5.1	13.6
21	4.59	3.90	3.61	3.76	4.11	3.26	3.98	23.1	17.1	6.1	21.6	11.1	8.3	12.7
22	5.42	4.22	3.06	3.48	4.61	3.32	2.94	22.8	19.8	3.2	20.9	17.0	6.9	9.5
23	4.85	3.35	4.00	4.21	4.21	3.45	3.06	19.3	18.0	8.0	21.0	13.3	6.8	13.5
24	4.57	3.60	4.50	3.84	3.77	3.29	3.09	27.1	16.9	8.5	19.8	9.9	6.7	11.1
25	4.85	3.41	3.47	4.04	3.68	3.33	3.33	28.0	14.5	7.9	20.2	16.8	8.1	4.5
26	4.35	3.51	3.86	3.81	3.89	3.35	3.41	22.8	16.6	6.2	20.5	12.5	7.4	13.9
27	4.76	3.70	4.29	3.71	3.84	3.45	2.72	23.1	19.0	7.3	17.1	12.6	6.9	13.9
28	4.43	3.64	2.94	3.94	4.05	3.29	2.95	24.0	16.0	4.9	19.6	17.2	8.1	10.0
29	4.80	3.46	4.30	3.58	3.81	2.80	2.81	20.7	17.7	8.7	13.0	11.4	5.8	14.6
30	4.16	3.45	3.85	3.82	3.22	3.32	2.79	23.0	15.5	9.6	19.9	10.6	9.4	12.0
Average	5.29	4.21	4.34	4.16	4.25	3.38	3.37	22.4	19.4	7.7	17.7	12.6	7.4	12.8

4. Towns with Turnover of £19m. and under £30m.

Town Ref. No.‡	Sales per Person Engaged £'000†							Percentage of Total Sales for Town						
	G. & P.D.	O.F.	C.T. N.	C. & F.	H.G.	O.N. F.	G.S.	G. & P.D.	O.F.	C.T. N.	C. & F.	H.G.	O.N. F.	G.S.
1	6.62	5.46	6.08	5.16	4.54	3.98	3.36	23.8	24.1	11.4	16.6	10.5	7.6	5.9
2	6.67	4.84	5.37	5.61	5.67	3.45	3.44	20.4	19.5	7.5	21.6	13.9	6.6	10.5
3	6.76	4.64	5.50	5.34	5.02	3.68	3.28	23.1	19.7	8.2	17.4	13.4	7.5	10.6
4	5.99	5.14	5.13	5.31	4.52	3.91	3.33	16.5	16.5	8.2	21.6	12.7	8.5	15.9
5	5.84	4.26	4.62	4.67	4.44	3.97	4.41	24.0	18.2	7.7	18.7	11.4	7.1	12.8
6	5.61	5.27	3.83	4.60	4.56	4.01	3.63	20.9	17.1	5.5	19.9	15.7	9.6	11.3
7	5.85	4.38	5.18	5.61	4.12	3.80	3.19	22.3	17.1	6.9	20.8	18.2	7.4	7.4
8	5.76	5.01	5.52	4.91	3.98	3.48	3.41	20.5	19.4	7.9	18.8	11.5	8.1	13.7
9	5.36	4.60	5.33	4.58	4.84	3.78	3.45	19.8	21.9	9.7	16.9	16.3	6.8	8.7
10	6.41	4.93	5.60	4.13	4.32	3.89	2.94	22.6	26.1	11.3	15.7	10.3	10.5	3.5
11	5.89	4.43	4.68	4.70	4.08	4.34	3.37	19.5	15.5	5.6	16.7	13.7	13.0	16.1
12	6.30	4.94	6.21	3.93	4.22	3.48	3.32	22.7	26.2	14.0	10.8	15.3	6.7	4.2
13	4.84	4.27	5.03	4.74	4.02	3.57	3.64	22.0	14.9	7.9	25.3	12.4	7.6	9.9
14	4.91	4.77	3.94	4.84	3.85	3.37	3.56	21.3	27.4	6.2	16.9	11.6	6.2	10.4
15	5.64	4.46	6.09	4.18	4.04	3.30	2.89	20.2	23.0	11.1	15.0	11.7	6.0	12.9
16	5.81	4.20	4.19	3.39	4.41	3.43	3.75	20.0	17.5	6.2	29.3	12.9	5.3	8.6
17	4.86	3.56	5.97	4.12	4.46	3.06	3.61	20.2	16.3	8.1	20.1	16.7	6.8	11.5
18	4.98	4.32	4.09	3.66	3.55	3.25	4.78	21.2	17.7	7.2	19.4	13.8	8.3	12.4
19	5.64	4.47	4.26	4.10	3.37	3.23	3.23	19.2	23.1	8.3	15.3	14.3	8.4	11.3
20	5.46	4.04	3.56	4.00	4.06	3.29	3.21	21.9	21.0	6.0	17.4	11.9	7.1	14.6
21	4.68	4.18	3.58	4.07	3.90	3.82	3.18	24.4	16.1	7.1	18.6	14.5	8.0	11.4
22	4.55	3.84	4.40	4.27	4.11	3.32	3.06	24.8	15.7	7.1	16.9	9.0	5.8	20.6
23	4.53	3.67	3.87	4.06	3.77	3.07	3.70	26.8	17.1	8.3	19.1	12.8	7.6	8.4
24	4.25	3.98	3.98	4.09	3.68	3.16	3.53	20.7	16.9	8.4	24.9	12.5	8.0	8.7
25	4.98	3.79	3.66	3.85	3.61	3.23	3.44	23.2	16.8	6.9	17.2	15.6	7.8	12.6
26	4.91	3.77	4.07	4.06	3.80	2.80	3.23	19.1	14.7	6.2	21.2	11.9	11.3	15.5
27	4.79	3.76	4.09	3.45	3.87	3.28	3.65	19.7	16.1	6.4	22.5	13.5	9.8	12.0
28	4.24	4.04	4.48	3.91	3.80	3.35	2.96	18.2	15.9	5.4	21.5	10.0	8.9	20.0
29	4.37	3.70	4.06	3.97	3.84	3.18	3.24	22.4	19.7	6.9	15.4	14.9	6.9	13.9
30	4.91	3.42	4.49	3.65	3.57	2.83	3.74	22.7	20.6	10.1	13.1	10.0	6.7	16.9
31	4.41	3.64	3.18	3.78	3.85	3.01	4.11	27.1	15.2	6.9	19.5	14.9	7.8	8.7
32	4.34	3.50	3.26	3.55	3.62	3.04	3.44	26.8	17.3	8.8	19.3	15.9	7.4	4.5
33	4.68	3.76	3.98	3.14	3.60	2.93	2.88	32.3	23.2	11.7	12.6	11.7	6.1	2.5
34	4.22	3.50	2.88	3.64	3.34	2.93	3.61	27.2	16.1	7.3	18.6	15.2	7.6	8.0
Average	5.27	4.25	4.53	4.27	4.07	3.42	3.46	22.3	18.9	8.0	18.7	13.3	7.8	11.1

5. Towns with Turnover of £30m. and over

Town Ref. No.‡	Sales per Person Engaged £'000†							Percentage of Total Sales for Town						
	G. & P.D.	O.F.	C.T. N.	C. & F.	H.G.	O.N. F.	G.S.	G. & P.D.	O.F.	C. & N.	O. & F.	H.G.	O.N. F.	G.S.
1	6.49	5.15	5.49	4.49	4.12	3.67	3.23	20.9	23.9	10.2	13.8	10.7	7.5	13.0
2	5.61	4.64	4.35	5.16	4.23	3.89	3.60	17.2	18.1	5.9	15.7	13.4	7.8	21.9
3	5.05	4.99	4.08	4.46	4.43	3.74	4.00	14.9	21.8	5.9	20.1	12.0	7.1	18.2
4	5.31	4.73	4.73	4.19	4.22	3.53	3.96	23.3	21.3	7.4	15.5	11.8	6.7	14.1
5	6.28	5.02	5.32	3.87	4.31	3.67	3.21	23.5	23.0	12.1	11.6	13.4	8.2	8.2
6	6.02	4.77	4.92	4.29	4.21	3.46	3.14	22.0	19.6	9.2	18.2	15.6	6.6	8.9
7	5.23	4.60	4.91	4.47	4.06	3.53	3.52	20.4	22.5	8.7	17.0	10.7	6.8	13.9
8	5.47	4.07	4.24	4.50	3.93	3.33	3.98	16.4	16.4	9.7	22.1	13.1	10.2	12.0
9	4.95	4.27	4.06	4.39	4.29	3.80	3.56	23.5	15.6	7.6	17.9	12.1	7.6	15.7
10	5.35	4.43	3.80	4.14	4.44	3.24	3.54	22.8	21.3	6.0	19.0	14.0	6.9	9.9
11	5.77	4.34	4.37	3.95	3.93	3.10	3.54	19.1	22.4	9.5	16.1	14.6	7.5	10.7
12	4.84	3.97	4.43	5.12	4.22	3.44	3.28	16.5	14.1	5.3	19.4	11.4	7.6	25.7
13	5.27	4.40	3.65	4.40	4.00	3.36	3.44	21.8	21.0	5.9	18.6	12.4	7.5	12.9
14	4.79	4.03	4.55	4.59	3.81	3.63	3.21	19.2	15.7	8.7	19.8	10.8	7.6	18.1
15	5.16	3.99	3.97	4.37	3.73	3.08	3.56	21.1	16.1	6.7	19.5	13.7	7.9	15.0
16	4.87	4.20	4.68	4.20	4.01	3.46	3.10	17.6	15.3	7.4	19.5	10.1	9.1	21.0
17	4.37	4.13	3.80	4.53	3.90	3.60	3.48	20.6	13.1	6.5	22.4	10.8	8.0	18.5
18	4.97	4.17	3.70	3.85	3.28	2.92	3.39	20.8	18.1	8.1	17.6	11.7	6.1	17.5
19	5.12	4.46	3.71	4.45	3.74	3.34	2.92	20.7	18.5	7.1	15.6	10.5	7.1	20.4
20	4.64	4.19	4.43	3.89	3.87	3.21	3.34	21.1	20.6	8.0	16.9	11.1	8.0	14.3
21	4.34	4.02	4.06	4.13	3.76	3.13	3.64	19.5	19.5	8.8	18.1	10.6	9.9	13.5
22	4.87	3.80	4.24	3.87	3.59	3.29	3.43	18.4	16.2	5.8	20.9	13.9	9.7	15.0
23	5.21	3.43	4.56	4.17	3.41	3.29	3.28	20.4	18.1	8.0	19.4	11.5	8.1	14.5
24	4.55	3.57	5.25	4.39	3.41	3.24	3.28	18.6	16.5	9.8	15.5	10.5	6.8	22.2
25	4.42	3.91	3.93	3.95	4.05	3.35	3.21	24.8	18.2	7.2	16.2	11.7	7.4	14.4
26	4.81	3.52	5.03	4.09	3.54	3.27	3.20	20.9	15.7	11.0	19.3	11.3	6.8	14.9
27	4.66	3.68	3.94	4.02	3.60	3.07	3.46	25.5	16.6	7.1	15.1	10.3	6.3	19.1
28	4.48	3.84	3.92	4.29	3.32	3.02	3.47	18.7	19.4	5.4	14.5	9.5	6.7	25.9
29	4.94	4.05	4.32	3.93	3.40	3.26	2.93	17.9	18.2	7.4	16.4	11.0	8.5	20.5
30	4.90	3.87	4.09	3.96	4.11	3.25	2.64	26.1	14.5	9.0	16.9	14.3	7.6	11.6
31	4.71	3.72	3.36	3.81	3.65	3.12	3.19	28.2	15.9	7.0	15.5	11.4	7.5	14.6
32	5.20	3.37	3.88	3.92	3.50	3.03	3.08	21.8	21.4	7.4	20.5	11.4	7.8	9.8
33	4.67	3.29	3.90	3.83	3.81	3.01	3.10	21.6	12.9	7.9	15.6	10.2	6.0	25.0
34	4.76	2.89	3.96	3.64	3.52	2.95	2.90	26.2	13.9	8.8	17.4	10.8	6.1	16.8
Average	5.06	4.10	4.28	4.22	3.86	3.33	3.35	20.9	18.1	7.8	17.6	11.8	7.6	16.1

Appendix D
Productivity Ranking of Towns: Overall and by Form of Organisation

(a) Town Size-Classes (1)-(3)

| | Class of Towns | | | | | |
| | (1) | | (2) | | (3) | |
Overall Ranking	Independents	Multiples & Cooperatives	Independents	Multiples & Cooperatives	Independents	Multiples & Co-operatives
1	6	1	1	4	3	2
2	1	6	7	1	6	1
3	5	4	5	3	1	6
4	7	3	2	5	4	3
5	4	7	3	6	5	10
6	2	8	4	16	8	5
7	8	2	6	9	11	7
8	14	11	17	8	9	9
9	10	5	10	12	2	11
10	3	12	15	2	10	4
11	9	9	11	15	7	13
12	13	10	22	10	12	18
13	11	16	14	14	19	8
14	12	15	13	7	23	12
15	16	14	9	21	13	21
16	18	13	21	13	25	14
17	17	17	12	19	14	19
18	15	20	8	28	16	17
19	19	28	25	11	22	24
20	29	19	16	23	30	15
21	26	21	23	24	20	20
22	22	25	20	22	27	22
23	24	22	19	17	26	16
24	27	23	18	30	15	27
25	21	18	24	20	21	28
26	25	26	26	29	18	26
27	20	29	28	18	29	23
28	28	27	30	26	24	29
29	23	31	29	27	17	30
30	30	24	27	31	28	25
31	31	30	31	25		

Note   The figures in the first column refer to the ranking of towns in descending order of unadjusted sales per person engaged (full-time equivalent). The figures in the other columns show for each size-class the rank order of each town according to the average sales per person engaged of (a) its independent shops and (b) its multiples and co-operatives. The identity of each town is found by referring to the second column of Appendix B. Thus in size-class 1 the town with the highest unadjusted sales per person engaged is Surbiton; it also has the highest unadjusted sales per person engaged for multiples and cooperatives but ranks sixth for independents.

(b) Town Size-Classes (4) and (5)

| | Class of Towns | | | |
| | (4) | | (5) | |
Overall Ranking	Independents	Multiples & Cooperatives	Independents	Multiples & Co-operatives
1	2	2	7	1
2	9	1	2	4
3	3	8	4	7
4	1	10	1	12
5	5	6	3	3
6	8	5	5	11
7	16	3	6	10
8	14	4	16	2
9	4	12	8	8
10	7	7	20	5
11	13	15	9	9
12	11	19	11	6
13	10	21	27	17
14	15	17	23	13
15	6	28	12	16
16	12	31	15	18
17	17	25	10	26
18	21	9	17	19
19	20	16	14	30
20	26	11	21	20
21	19	14	13	29
22	24	18	24	14
23	27	22	25	21
24	22	32	28	24
25	28	27	22	22
26	30	23	29	15
27	32	13	19	32
28	18	29	30	28
29	31	26	18	31
30	23	30	34	25
31	25	33	31	27
32	29	34	32	23
33	33	20	26	34
34	34	24	33	33

Appendix E
Productivity Ranking of Towns:
Overall and by Kind of Business

1. Towns with Sales of £10m. and under £12.25m.

	Ranking Order by Kind of Business						
Overall Ranking	Grocers	Other Food	Confectioners Tobacconists Newsagents	Clothing and Footwear	Household Goods	Other Non Food	General Stores
1	1	1	6	25	12	13	13
2	3	10	5	5	1	11	23
3	4	3	3	12	11	15	19
4	6	2	17	3	2	6	3
5	8	6	13	21	8	2	21
6	7	4	2	13	9	3	4
7	10	9	11	2	6	1	7
8	2	5	16	1	15	5	29
9	5	12	1	23	10	18	20
10	9	8	9	16	20	17	28
11	15	7	12	27	21	8	8
12	16	13	4	17	26	7	9
13	11	11	10	28	7	20	31
14	14	16	21	10	4	4	15
15	23	15	15	29	5	25	25
16	12	18	18	4	3	12	26
17	28	20	8	9	17	16	5
18	17	25	7	6	16	14	18
19	18	19	29	22	18	28	11
20	25	14	31	19	13	10	17
21	13	21	30	18	25	26	22
22	29	26	14	7	19	22	21
23	21	17	25	14	27	19	6
24	19	24	19	8	31	31	10
25	20	22	27	30	28	21	14
26	24	23	26	31	14	29	16
27	26	27	22	11	23	27	27
28	22	31	24	20	22	9	12
29	31	28	20	15	30	23	24
30	30	29	28	24	24	30	1
31	27	30	23	26	29	24	30

Note The figures in the first column refer to the ranking of towns in descending order
unadjusted sales per person engaged (full-time equivalent). The figures in the c
columns show the rank order of each town according to the average sales per p
son engaged of its shops in each kind of business. The identity of each town is f
by referring to the second column of Table 2. Thus Surbiton has the highest ov
(unadjusted) sales per person engaged. It is also ranked first for Groceries and
Provisions and Other Food, but is ranked sixth for the Confections, Tobacconist
Newsagents group, etc.

. Towns with Sales of £12.25m. and under £15m.

Overall Ranking	Grocers	Other Food	Confectioners Tobacconists Newsagents	Clothing and Footwear	Household Goods	Other Non Food	General Stores
1	4	7	1	14	13	6	16
2	5	2	2	1	1	12	9
3	2	6	7	13	9	8	7
4	1	11	4	18	3	14	17
5	8	4	9	10	2	9	28
6	12	14	5	6	6	1	13
7	3	5	8	24	18	4	21
8	9	8	21	4	5	11	11
9	20	1	23	12	20	7	1
10	6	9	6	2	7	27	29
11	13	15	12	7	8	21	4
12	14	24	22	9	12	5	3
13	18	13	29	15	4	16	5
14	7	10	3	11	17	20	26
15	15	18	18	8	14	2	10
16	11	23	13	3	21	3	14
17	10	12	14	30	22	22	18
18	24	17	10	26	15	17	24
19	16	3	16	20	11	19	25
20	26	22	15	21	10	18	15
21	25	29	19	28	25	29	2
22	19	27	20	5	26	28	8
23	30	19	26	22	19	15	6
24	21	21	30	16	16	24	27
25	28	16	11	23	28	10	20
26	23	20	17	19	30	13	22
27	22	26	25	31	24	31	23
28	29	28	31	29	23	23	31
29	17	30	27	25	31	30	19
30	31	25	28	27	29	26	12
31	27	31	24	17	27	25	30

3. Towns with Sales of £15m. and under £19m.

	Ranking Order by Kind of Business						
Overall Ranking	Grocers	Other Food	Confectioners Tobacconists Newsagents	Clothing and Footwear	Household Goods	Other Non Food	General Store
1	1	7	7	1	5	10	2
2	17	10	6	29	1	27	19
3	18	2	14	5	4	2	5
4	2	9	2	10	6	3	7
5	5	4	1	3	7	6	17
6	3	3	17	12	21	28	1
7	7	1	8	2	25	1	10
8	6	15	10	4	8	7	13
9	4	11	4	20	17	15	20
10	8	8	5	19	13	5	12
11	14	12	3	25	14	23	23
12	11	6	21	22	12	16	9
13	21	5	18	6	9	25	15
14	15	19	26	17	23	12	8
15	20	18	23	13	19	13	4
16	13	26	22	15	18	30	6
17	19	13	9	8	2	4	24
18	10	14	11	14	10	11	16
19	9	16	13	11	16	24	25
20	12	17	29	30	3	19	27
21	26	21	27	26	15	25	3
22	16	20	19	7	22	17	18
23	22	29	28	16	29	18	14
24	23	30	20	9	11	8	22
25	27	24	12	21	28	21	21
26	29	25	24	24	24	14	11
27	28	23	30	18	20	22	26
28	25	22	16	27	26	9	30
29	24	27	15	28	27	29	28
30	30	28	25	23	30	20	29

Towns with Sales of £19m. and under £30m.

Ranking Order by Kind of Business

verall anking	Grocers	Other Food	Confectioners Tobacconists Newsagents	Clothing and Footwear	Household Goods	Other Non Food	General Stores
	3	1	3	5	5	3	20
	2	7	8	1	1	14	16
	1	9	7	3	2	10	23
	5	5	1	24	11	13	22
	4	6	5	15	10	6	32
	9	17	14	10	8	4	2
	8	14	1C	2	12	8	28
	6	3	11	4	6	5	21
	16	10	9	12	3	9	14
	14	2	28	11	4	2	9
	11	4	6	6	18	12	18
	7	13	13	9	14	1	19
	23	16	12	8	17	11	8
	21	8	26	7	22	16	12
	12	12	2	14	16	19	33
	22	31	4	16	7	28	10
	17	15	20	28	32	22	1
	10	18	19	33	9	15	4
	13	11	18	17	33	24	25
	15	21	31	22	15	20	27
	26	19	30	19	19	7	29
	28	29	27	21	26	27	6
	32	22	24	18	27	26	13
	27	23	17	13	13	18	30
	18	24	29	26	29	23	15
	20	34	15	29	31	33	5
	29	30	33	27	21	30	3
	25	26	25	34	30	32	34
	24	27	21	32	20	21	7
	30	28	23	23	23	25	24
	19	25	22	20	24	34	26
	33	20	16	25	25	17	31
	31	33	32	31	28	29	17
	34	32	34	30	34	31	11

5. Towns with Sales of £30m. and over

Ranking Order by Kind of Business

Overall Ranking	Grocers	Other Food	Confectioners Tobacconists Newsagents	Clothing and Footwear	Household Goods	Other Non Food	General Stores
1	1	1	1	6	9	4	21
2	2	2	2	29	3	5	22
3	3	4	5	15	8	10	27
4	8	5	7	17	6	9	3
5	15	3	19	8	2	3	1
6	5	6	14	1	5	1	5
7	10	7	6	7	11	8	10
8	7	9	29	19	1	23	8
9	17	12	21	11	4	2	6
10	6	17	17	5	16	16	2
11	9	10	33	10	14	13	14
12	4	11	13	24	15	27	9
13	22	22	11	2	7	12	20
14	13	21	22	13	23	28	7
15	24	19	10	3	19	6	23
16	33	16	30	4	17	7	11
17	29	14	12	28	18	24	17
18	20	13	8	16	13	11	29
19	14	8	31	9	22	15	32
20	34	20	20	20	21	25	4
21	23	30	4	21	27	19	25
22	19	24	18	23	10	21	34
23	32	23	25	25	12	14	24
24	11	31	9	18	30	18	18
25	28	28	24	22	25	29	13
26	21	26	16	30	26	17	15
27	30	29	3	12	31	22	19
28	16	15	32	31	34	34	16
29	26	27	34	33	24	26	26
30	31	25	26	14	33	31	12
31	12	32	28	27	29	30	30
32	18	18	15	26	32	20	31
33	27	33	27	32	20	32	28
34	25	34	23	34	28	33	33

Main Data for Regression Analysis: All Retail Sales

. Towns with Sales of £10m. and under £12.25m.

Town ref. No. ||	Standardised Sales/Person Engaged (FTE)†	% Part-time Workers	% Vacancies minus % Unemployed*	Income/ head	Standardised Sales/Shop**	% Sales due to Mult. & Co-ops
1	4808	33	1.4	784	25,000	60.2
2	4717	32	1.3	767	23,256	49.3
3	4695	34	0.3	743	22,222	55.9
4	4695	37	1.6	784	21,739	53.7
5	4608	35	1.5	758	20,833	59.7
6	4608	33	2.2	758	22,727	68.5
7	4587	38	1.6	784	23,256	61.1
8	4525	34	1.0	715	21,739	54.4
9	4367	32	1.9	784	16,667	47.9
10	4348	21	0.5	715	22,727	49.8
11	4310	25	0.2	777	17,544	49.9
12	4274	36	1.0	715	18.519	51.9
13	4219	33	0.9	759	16,667	46.3
14	4219	30	2.4	758	19,608	46.0
15	4132	21	0.6	705	20,833	44.9
16	4132	28	1.8	777	20,833	40.4
17	4049	31	0.2	743	15,152	60.7
18	4032	25	0.6	702	21,739	53.7
19	3984	30	1.0	734	12,658	45.2
20	3922	29	1.1	691	17,857	63.3
21	3906	29	1.1	734	14,286	46.2
22	3906	27	0.6	689	18,182	57.4
23	3861	28	0.1	711	13,699	58.8
24	3861	19	−1.6	657	18,868	57.8
25	3774	18	−0.1	654	23,256	47.5
26	3759	25	−1.3	734	12,987	45.7
27	3690	27	−2.5	708	14,925	48.1
28	3663	21	−1.8	654	21,277	46.9
29	3663	21	−6.8	686	18,519	62.0
30	3559	25	−2.0	708	12,987	46.5
31	3472	21	−0.7	670	22,222	44.5
Average	4157	29	0.3	729	19,159	52.5

‖ Equal to rank order for standardised sales per person engaged.

† Sales per person engaged adjusted to take account of differences between towns in proportion of sales made by individual kinds of business.

* Average 1957-1961.

** Sales per shop adjusted to take account of differences between towns in proportion of sales made by individual kinds of business.

2. Towns with Sales of £12.25m. and under £15m.

Town Ref. No. ‖	Standardised Sales/Person Engaged (FTE)†	% Part-time Workers	% Vacancies minus % Unemployed*	Income/ head	Standardised Sales/Shop**	% Sales due to Mult. & Co-ops
1	4926	31	3.1	764	24,390	60.7
2	4695	31	3.2	784	21,277	53.8
3	4630	28	0.4	743	22,222	60.1
4	4484	32	1.5	784	18,868	49.7
5	4464	27	1.0	743	20,000	56.8
6	4444	25	0.8	715	22,222	68.0
7	4425	34	1.0	743	17,857	49.2
8	4425	28	0.8	731	15,385	58.2
9	4424	26	1.3	743	22,727	53.6
10	4386	37	1.4	784	19,608	53.6
11	4348	28	1.1	758	19,608	49.3
12	4329	26	0.3	715	20,408	57.7
13	4274	25	0.5	715	21,739	55.0
14	4219	18	−2.8	677	19,231	65.0
15	4219	23	0.7	706	14,706	62.2
16	4184	23	0.1	715	22,222	50.6
17	4167	23	0.7	743	22,222	59.9
18	3968	25	0.2	706	17,241	49.4
19	3937	28	0.2	730	17,241	43.0
20	3906	25	0.2	715	16,393	51.7
21	3891	22	0.9	654	14,286	50.2
22	3831	28	−2.1	715	18,182	42.6
23	3817	31	−0.4	708	10,638	42.1
24	3817	24	−3.0	670	16,393	57.6
25	3817	19	1.3	666	19,231	53.3
26	3636	27	−1.2	670	12,821	60.6
27	3546	25	−0.9	706	14,085	48.1
28	3521	28	−4.5	701	11,494	48.8
29	3559	19	1.0	690	14,493	44.1
30	3509	29	−1.3	708	8,696	35.1
31	3333	17	−3.5	680	10,101	49.6
Average	4119	27	0.1	720	17,767	53.0

3. Towns with Sales of £15m. and under £19m.

Town Ref. No. ‖	Standardised Sales/Person Engaged (FTE)†	% Part-time Workers	% Vacancies minus % Unemployed*	Income/ head	Standardised Sales/Shop**	% Sales due to Mult. & Co-ops
1	5076	37	2. 7	784	23, 256	68. 8
2	4739	28	1. 9	758	30, 303	62. 2
3	4630	32	1. 4	784	20, 000	54. 7
4	4630	36	1. 5	784	23, 810	65. 0
5	4608	29	0. 3	759	17, 857	50. 4
6	4587	31	0. 7	715	23, 256	63. 6
7	4425	31	1. 6	787	23, 256	54. 8
8	4367	32	1. 0	743	16, 949	49. 2
9	4348	34	2. 2	784	17, 241	51. 5
10	4292	33	1. 5	784	16, 667	40. 2
11	4255	26	0. 7	691	18, 868	50. 1
12	4237	25	1. 3	731	22, 222	57. 4
13	4237	30	1. 2	715	22, 727	50. 7
14	4219	24	−0. 9	670	18, 182	53. 9
15	4132	31	1. 0	743	14, 085	43. 8
16	4115	26	0. 8	702	22, 222	61. 5
17	4098	27	1. 1	691	19, 608	53. 5
18	4065	26	0. 1	715	18, 868	53. 4
19	4032	26	−0. 4	708	15, 625	52. 9
20	3984	23	−2. 3	708	14, 085	52. 5
21	3953	22	−0. 5	715	16, 393	50. 2
22	3891	22	−1. 1	708	16, 949	70. 2
23	3861	27	0. 2	687	16, 129	46. 3
24	3802	29	−3. 2	686	21, 739	55. 4
25	3788	31	0. 4	715	13, 889	43. 7
26	3774	26	−1. 7	708	13, 889	39. 7
27	3745	24	−0. 1	670	16, 667	56. 1
28	3676	23	−0. 1	704	16, 949	52. 6
29	3636	28	−4. 3	670	15, 625	48. 0
30	3521	26	−0. 2	708	15, 625	40. 5
Average	4158	28	0. 2	724	18, 765	53. 1

4. Towns with Sales of £19m. and under £30m.

Town Ref. No. ‖	Standardised Sales/Person Engaged (FTE)†	% Part-time Workers	% Vacancies minus % Unemployed*	Income/ head	Standardised Sales/Shop**	% Sales due to Mult. & Co-ops
1	5025	36	3.7	784	25,000	63.6
2	5025	30	1.0	743	25,641	68.2
3	4878	36	1.2	767	32,258	66.4
4	4831	33	1.9	764	25,000	61.8
5	4651	29	0.9	787	20,408	59.8
6	4630	28	1.6	796	27,027	53.8
7	4608	25	1.2	715	30,303	65.0
8	4608	32	2.4	758	23,810	67.5
9	4566	28	1.0	743	19,608	53.0
10	4525	32	2.6	784	22,727	56.3
11	4525	26	1.4	695	24,390	58.6
12	4505	28	1.9	784	19,608	48.0
13	4329	26	—0.4	696	19,608	54.9
14	4292	25	0.6	734	17,241	58.8
15	4255	27	1.0	743	15,625	45.1
16	4167	26	1.1	709	23,810	45.4
17	4098	23	0.8	715	17,241	54.5
18	4098	29	0.7	725	15,873	48.3
19	4098	25	1.0	706	21,277	49.7
20	4032	22	—0.4	668	22,222	48.6
21	4000	34	0.7	715	14,493	43.1
22	4000	23	—1.7	690	18,182	58.3
23	3876	31	0.5	711	12,048	43.4
24	3876	26	—0.3	708	12,987	48.0
25	3876	28	—0.1	690	16,949	48.0
26	3876	21	—0.2	666	20,408	49.0
27	3861	27	0.1	702	20,000	49.2
28	3846	22	—0.1	711	20,408	52.4
29	3817	27	—0.4	691	14,085	42.5
30	3788	24	—3.1	711	13,333	49.0
31	3774	27	—0.2	708	11,904	44.4
32	3610	29	—1.2	708	10,101	37.7
33	3571	27	—0.1	708	10,204	32.3
34	3534	29	—0.4	708	9,434	39.9

5. Towns with Sales of £30m. and over

Town Ref. No. ‖	Standardised Sales/Person Engaged (FTE)†	% Part-time Workers	% Vacancies minus % Unemployed*	Income/ head	Standardised Sales/Shop**	% Sales due to Mult. & Co-ops
1	4545	34	1.5	784	23,810	56.9
2	4505	28	1.6	747	25,641	65.1
3	4464	27	0.1	759	21,277	47.0
4	4405	30	0.2	777	18,868	50.8
5	4386	36	0.8	784	23,810	54.6
6	4329	31	0.6	743	25,000	59.1
7	4329	29	0.2	759	18,519	57.9
8	4274	26	0.0	706	19,608	53.7
9	4219	29	0.3	720	17,857	52.2
10	4184	29	0.1	704	18,519	51.0
11	4149	26	0.2	743	19,608	47.7
12	4149	20	—0.8	708	23,810	63.7
13	4132	29	0.8	767	16,949	52.4
14	4049	25	—0.1	708	15,873	51.8
15	4032	29	0.2	706	16,949	52.6
16	4032	25	0.5	692	18,868	46.3
17	4016	21	—2.2	692	18,182	50.6
18	4000	23	—0.6	702	18,868	63.0
19	3968	25	—1.1	702	23,810	65.3
20	3937	28	—0.1	702	18,182	51.9
21	3922	21	—0.3	708	16,667	46.5
22	3891	22	—0.8	654	21,739	45.9
23	3861	27	—0.7	706	21,739	55.3
24	3861	26	—2.7	708	17,544	58.4
25	3840	26	0.3	715	16,393	51.2
26	3831	24	—2.4	658	21,277	55.4
27	3817	26	—1.6	690	16,949	43.1
28	3817	21	—1.8	666	19,231	57.1
29	3802	23	0.3	702	20,000	49.9
30	3759	31	0.0	708	14,706	41.7
31	3704	26	—0.1	734	13,158	43.2
32	3704	18	—2.2	646	23,810	54.6
33	3650	26	—3.5	670	18,182	46.4
34	3448	27	—4.4	690	18,519	48.7